TRUTH

AN ESSAY IN
MORAL RECONSTRUCTION

T0382345

TRUTH

AN ESSAY IN MORAL
RECONSTRUCTION

BY

SIR CHARLES WALSTON (WALDSTEIN)

CAMBRIDGE
AT THE UNIVERSITY PRESS
1919

Truth is one of the greatest material assets in the
life of a nation and must be directly guarded and
developed as are Life and Property.

Freedom of the Press does not mean freedom to
disseminate lies and errors.

CAMBRIDGE
UNIVERSITY PRESS

University Printing House, Cambridge CB2 8BS, United Kingdom

Cambridge University Press is part of the University of Cambridge.

It furthers the University's mission by disseminating knowledge in the pursuit of
education, learning and research at the highest international levels of excellence.

www.cambridge.org
Information on this title: www.cambridge.org/9781107505742

© Cambridge University Press 1919

First published 1919
First paperback edition 2015

A catalogue record for this publication is available from the British Library

ISBN 978-1-107-50574-2 Paperback

PREFACE

THIS ESSAY (which is a supplement to my earlier book *Aristodemocracy*) was written during the autumn and winter of 1917–18. For various reasons, its publication has been delayed. Though the actual war has ended, this momentous change has not affected the purpose and the arguments of the book. In spite of the influence and supreme importance of economic causes which prepared for the inception and continuance of the war, as they affect the terms of peace and will dominate the civilised world for some time to come, I maintain now, as I expressed my opinions from the beginning, that the efficient cause of the war is to be found in the defective moral standards and moral education of the civilised world, and that Moral Reconstruction is at least as urgently needed as is industrial and financial re-adjustment.

The immediate influence of the war—in spite of all the heroism and self-sacrifice which it has evoked in millions of patriotic citizens—has been to lower the moral standards of the world, already defective and anachronistic before the war. To the previous inadequacies and defects of our ethical systems and education in pre-war times must now be added, among minor symptoms of degeneration, the lowering and coarsening of our sense of the value of human life, a necessary, almost logical sequence to all wars; the growth of thriftlessness and profligacy owing to the unsettling of economic and financial standards and the suspension of the laws and regulations governing contracts

and, in many cases, the acquisition of surplus income to
those not accustomed to such affluence; and, above all, the
lowering of the standards of Truth. This increase of untruthfulness is not only caused by the general derangement
of social life and the unbalancing of nerves among the
majority of the population, as well as by the growth of
more or less justified suspiciousness against one's neighbours, when spying and illicit dealing with the enemy exist
and must be forcibly counteracted; but it is, above all,
encouraged, if not produced, by the recognised use of
deception and trickery of all kinds as a legitimate method
of warfare. The last and most distasteful outcome is the
introduction into our vernacular of that hateful word
"camouflage," used with nauseating frequency and grati-
fication by even the most illiterate. Camouflage is the
attempt at deception—lying—not by words, but by means
of objects. It is an extension of untruthfulness which is a
recognised and legitimate form of warfare.

Thus the delay in the publication of this book has served
to present us with fresh conditions which demand even
more urgently than before the need for reconstruction of
our morals as regards truthfulness.

What concerns the life of the individual citizen applies
equally, if not more so, to public morality. The numerous
infringements of personal liberty and of higher spiritual
morality, made necessary by the pressing expediency of
war, have in innumerable cases, set expediency above
morality. The enactment by what has popularly been
summarised under the name of an interfering and not too
scrupulous "person" called "Dora," however justified by
the exceptional necessities of war, has not infrequently led

to the suppression of truth and even to the direct encouragement of deception. The activity of the Censorship, private and public, has tended in the same direction. Some time must elapse, even after the suspension of the censorship, for the tradition of scrupulous recognition of the sanctity of private information by word and in letters to be re-established among us, as well as the straightforward adherence to truth and nothing but the truth. The same applies emphatically to the great organ of publicity, the Press. Its power of suppressing facts and, positively, of producing "stunts," which, to say the least, present facts or whole groups of facts out of all proportion, has grown inordinately and asserted itself as a fixed tradition during this time of war. The crying need for action to regulate this most powerful and most dangerous institution in modern life, to which I have devoted much of the space in this book, can hardly be overstated.

In view of the fact that (page 98) I single out one of the leading journalists of the world to illustrate one of the most glaring defects in our system of publicity and the absurdity of established traditions as regards the personal and, at the same time, irresponsible power of such journalists, I desire here to bear testimony to the patriotic intentions of Lord Northcliffe and to the important work in many directions achieved by him during the war. It is possible that, in the future, history may confirm the claim which he may have established to the gratitude of the country. But the system itself remains wrong and a growing evil.

In the Appendix I have reprinted extracts from previous books and articles by me dealing with some of the subjects treated in the book itself. I have done this because I believe that it strengthens the argument to show that the same conclusions were arrived at in earlier years under essentially different conditions and from an independent point of view. But I should like to draw especial attention to the fact that the praise which was in earlier years bestowed upon the scientific spirit prevailing in German universities and in their whole educational system, applied to the Germany of old and not to the Germany of modern *Streberthum*. The advent of the latter *régime* I endeavoured to indicate in my book *Aristodemocracy*. The older spirit of scientific thoroughness, we hope, is not wholly dead even now. Its decline in more recent years has been pointed out on various occasions and quite recently by leading Germans of the "old school." This moral and intellectual degeneration began with Bismarck. I may claim to have recognised this process of degeneration in what I wrote about thirty years ago; but most clearly in my little book, *The Expansion of Western Ideals and the World's Peace*, published in 1899, from which I may be allowed to quote the following passages (pp. 139 seq.):

...But again there turned up a great man of action who, knowing his countrymen and the trend of the times, utilized all these currents to weld together the separate blocks,—smoothly polished and florid marbles of prince-ridden principalities and clumsy unhewn stones and rubble stones of independent cities or towns,—the huge edifice of the German Empire. The scientific spirit which was pervading the civilized world of Western Europe was recognised by Bismarck as a useful force which could be turned into practical advantage for the great purpose he had in view. He called upon the German professor—even the ethnologist, philologist and historian—and

they obeyed his commands with readiness and alacrity. The
theoretical and scientific lever with which these huge building
blocks were to be raised in order to construct the German
Empire was to be the scientific establishment of the unity of
the German people based upon the unity of Germanic races.
An historical basis for German unity was not enough; an
ethnological, racial unity had to be established. The historical
and philological literature of German University professors
belonging to the time of Bismarck's ascendancy, can almost be
recognised and classified by their relation to the problem of
establishing, fixing, and distinguishing from those of other
races, the laws and customs, literature, languages and religions,
the life and thought, the productions and aspirations of the
Germanic race....The distinctive feature in this modern
version of the old story of national lust of power is that it now
assumed a more serious and stately garb of historical justice in
the pedantic pretensions of its inaccurate ethnological theories.
The absurdity of any application of such ethnological theories
to the practical politics of modern nations at once becomes
manifest when an attempt is made to classify inhabitants of
any one of these western nations by means of such racial distinctions. What becomes of the racial unity of the present
German Empire if we consider the Slavs of Prussia, the Wends
in the North and the tangle of different racial occupations and
interminglings during the last thousand years within every
portion of the German country?...But the German professor
with his political brief wrapped round the lecture notes within
the oilcloth portfolio, pressed between his broadcloth sleeve and
ribs, as he walks to his lecture-room, was forced further afield
and deeper down in his "scientific" distinctions. The divisions
he established for the purposes of national policy were but
minor sub-divisions of broader ethnological distinctions. Here
the philologist took the lead and established "beyond all
doubt" the difference, nay, the antagonism, between the Arian
and Semitic, which makes the Hindoo more closely related to
the German and Saxon than these are to Spinoza, Mendelssohn
and Heine, Carl Marx and Disraeli....

Since Bismarck's time the falsification of humanistic studies, especially History and the "Science of *Politik*" to uphold the German theory of the State, of Autocracy, Bureaucracy, Militarism, as well as the "Ethics of Might," has been amply demonstrated in recent publications.

But, with the growth of *Real Politik* since Bismarck, the predominance of the one aim,—to increase material prosperity, industrial and commercial,—has led to the lowering of the purely scientific spirit of natural and physical science which formerly ruled their Universities and, through them, their whole educational system down to the elementary Schools. The University has been affected by the Polytechnic and Technical High School. Modern German *Streberthum* has effectually lowered the standards of their scientific and educational system, and this has of late years been admitted by the best representatives of German thought, who have had the courage to oppose the current of political and military domination responsible for this war. It is the *older* valuation of Theoretical Truth which *formerly* flourished in Germany from which we can learn. In the domain of Practical Truth, in political and social life, as developed by our political and social traditions and favoured by the spirit of fair-play in our national sports and pastimes, the Germans and all nations on the Continent of Europe can learn from us and from the people of the United States—in fact from all English-speaking nations.

I have gratefully to acknowledge the help given me in advice and criticism by various friends. My colleagues, Professor J. B. Bury and Mr N. Wedd, Fellows of King's College, Cambridge, as well as Mr Sydney Brooks (especially as regards the part dealing with Journalism and Publicity) have made most valuable suggestions. The same applies to my wife and to my friend, Mr George Leveson Gower, who have again helped me in seeing the book through the press; while my step-daughter, Dorothy Seligman, has given efficient secretarial help. I must also thank the Editor of the *Nineteenth Century and After* for the kind permission to reprint the article "The Kaiser and the 'Will to...' The need for universal Moral Reconstruction" which appeared in the January number of that review.

C. W.

NEWTON HALL, NEWTON,
    CAMBRIDGE.
        February, 1919.

CONTENTS

CHAP.   PAGE
VII.   THE IDEAL JOURNALIST   117
VIII. CRITICAL EXAMINATION OF THIS IDEAL OF
       JOURNALISM   122
IX.   "RECONSTRUCTION" OF JOURNALISM BY THE
       STATE   132
X.   "RECONSTRUCTION" OF JOURNALISM FROM WITH-
       IN   151

PART III.

RELIGIOUS TRUTH   157

APPENDIX
I.   THE IDEAL OF A UNIVERSITY   167
II.   SCIENCE AND EMPIRICISM, THEORY AND PRAC-
      TICE   182
III. EDUCATIONAL REFORM   194
IV.   MODESTY   199
V.   THE KAISER AND "THE WILL TO..."   .   .   213

TRUTH

INTRODUCTION

THE longer, and I may perhaps hope, the more enduring part of my book *Aristodemocracy*[1] is occupied with the attempted reconstruction of our ethical system. The essential and differentiating feature of this ethical system consists in the supreme demand which it puts forward for each period in the history of humanity—whether counted by decades or by centuries—to formulate anew and clearly, without bias and without being determined by existing religious dogmas and current social conventions, not only its own ethical codes, but also the summary ideal of man, the Ideal of the Gentleman. This is to ensure progress for humanity, i.e. normal moral, social and political evolution. But this evolution is not to be "*fatalistic*," i.e. entirely dependent upon forces of nature acting through the organism or the environment and leading to the survival of the fittest; but it is to be *Conscious Evolution*, i.e. guided by man's reason, his sense of truth and justice, his charity, even his sense of beauty—all these forces of the human mind permeating imagination, which is the motive, creative and progressive power in the human soul. This conscious ethical evolution is to be applied, not only to individual man, but also to social groups and to political organisations.

[1] *Aristodemocracy, From the Great War back to Moses, Christ and Plato*, London, 1916, New York, 1917.

Practical
Idealism and
Conscious
Evolution. If a definite name is to be given to this system of philosophy it had best be termed *Practical Idealism*, guided by *Conscious Evolution* and subordinated to the *Philosophy of Harmonism*. Its essence and importance, as a guide to human conduct, consist above all in the correct formulation and application of the right ultimate ideals. We are convinced that if these ultimate ideals (the final goal and beacon-light in man's wandering through life) are wrong, the whole journey loses its correct bearing and direction. Our ultimate ideals are thus of supreme practical importance even in individual and immediate action. But the recognition of this importance does not in any way lead us at once and prematurely to insist upon, or to expect, the realization of what is ultimate. Having determined the true nature and clear recognisability of his ideals, and fixed them as guiding stars for the distant future, man must concentrate his attention and his effort on the proximate ideals.

I might be allowed here to quote a passage from a previous work[1] where this same question is dealt with.

If it be thought, by some who pride themselves upon possessing a sober and practical mind, that these Expansionist ideals are rather vague and remote as forces which directly move the interested action of a nation, and have no power to check its aggressive action when passionate interest strongly urges it on in the wrong direction; if they doubt whether these ideals are sufficiently proximate and tangible to enter into the conscious life of the individual and to affect his actions, I will sin against the dictates of good taste and will make a personal confession, confident as I am that there are thousands who feel as I do.

So far from being remote and ineffectual, I solemnly declare

[1] *The Expansion of Western Ideals and the World's Peace*, London and New York, 1899, pp. 101 seq.

that these ideals with regard to the aims of Western civilisation form the foundation of my conscious existence even in the most practical aspects of my life. That, if I were not aware of their existence at the base of my consciousness, I could not pursue the vocation of life to which I have hitherto devoted myself, and by means of which I gain my subsistence. If I did not believe that ultimately all individual efforts culminate in the increase and strengthening, as well as in the diffusion, of Western civilisation and its highest and most subtle attainments, the best that man's intelligent effort has yet devised,—I should wish to spend my life in lotus-eating, if not to seek peace in Nirvana.

As I have arrived at this lofty sphere of aspiration, I will draw one last conclusion in the direction of ideals from the policy of Expansion as it ought to be followed by the United States; and I do this at the risk of being considered a "mere dreamer." But there are different kinds of dreamers; there are rational and irrational dreamers. Those who have succeeded in attaining the highest achievements in the world's history might all be called, and generally were called, dreamers. No man—and for that matter no nation—can do great things unless his imagination can produce, and hold up both before the intense discriminating power of his intellect, and before the untiring and unflinching energy of his will, some great ultimate goal to lofty endeavour. In so far all great men are idealists. But the difference between these idealists and the mere dreamers is that the latter spend their lives in the contemplation of their ideals, whereas to the former the ideals illuminate their lives. The dreamer gazes upon the brilliant sun until his vision is dimmed, and his whole brain lapses into an hypnotic state. The world outside the immediate radius of this brilliant sun is one great darkness, and he expends the weakened energy which is left to his somnolent nature in railing at this darkness and despising it. He is even unable to detect the lighter shades and half-tones, the infinite gradations which lie between the brilliancy of his distant sun and the darkness before and behind his feet. The idealist, on the other hand, having raised high aloft on the pinnacles of existence his brilliant beacon-light, does not spend his time in gazing immediately at it; but allows it to shed a lustre of illumination upon the whole roadway of life over which it shines; and instead of casting what is immediately at his feet into greater darkness, this distant light searches out every nook and cranny of existence, and enables him to pursue his path unfalteringly, to recognise the size and dimensions of each object in his path, its power of facilitating or impeding progress, of yielding or resisting; and, finally, it gives him a clear notion of distance itself. And thus he is patient, and not petulant, as regards what lies immediately before him, knowing that he has beyond a clear, lofty goal which lights and warms.

We must therefore insist upon the *real and practical* importance of establishing these correct ultimate ideals. Were we to attempt to express this in the old familiar terms in which humanity has embodied its highest general concepts we should say that Duty, including Justice, is the fundamental guide for human conduct in man's relation to himself, to humanity and to nature. It must be tempered by love or *Caritas* in his relation to his fellow-man, as well as for the good of his own soul, in order to give emotional initiative and direction leading to passion and enthusiasm. Above these, reigns Truth, which is the foundation of thought and action, in his social relationships as well as in his dealings with the world of things and nature; while Beauty gives him the sense of proportion, tempers and modifies all his thoughts and activities into a harmonious whole and leads his imagination on to a world of ideal perfection.

What we felt in insisting upon the need of the codification of modern morals has been put in the following terms[1]:

[1] *Aristodemocracy, From the Great War back to Moses, Christ and Plato*, London and New York, 1916 and 1917, pp. 200 seq.

What modern man and modern society require above all things is a clear and distinct codification of the moral consciousness of civilised man, not merely in a theoretical disquisition or in vague and general terms, which evade immediate application to the more complex or subtle needs of our daily life; but one which, arising out of the clear and unbiassed study of the actual problems of life, is fitted to meet every definite difficulty and to direct all moral effort towards one great and universally accepted end. It is the absence of such an ethical code, truly expressive of the best in us and accepted by all, and the means of bringing such a code to the knowledge of men, penetrating our educative system in its most elementary form as it applies even to the youngest children and is continuously impressed upon all people in every age of their life—it is the absence of such an effective system of moral education which lies at the root of all that is bad and irrational, not only in individual life, but in national life, and that has made this great war—at once barbarous, pedantically cruel, and unspeakably stupid—possible in modern times.

The reason why such an adequate expression of moral consciousness has not existed among us, in spite of the eminently practical and urgent need, is that the constitution and the teaching of ethics have been relegated to the sphere of theoretical study of principles, historical or speculative, and have not directly been concerned with establishing a practical guide to conduct. No real attempt has been made to draw up a code of ethics to meet the actual problems of daily life. Or, when thus considered in its immediate and practical bearings, this task has been relegated to the churches and the priests.

I there endeavoured to show, while insisting upon the necessity of religion, that though religion and ethics should never be divorced from each other, they envisage quite different spheres and can never replace each other.

I maintained that ethics with its immediately practical aims requires for its codification to be directly in touch with the needs of actual daily life, and has to be expressed with the greatest clearness, tested by correct observation, accurate as well as comprehensive, and by strict logic. I then endeavoured to present an outlined scheme for such a codification, summarising the several aspects under which ethical questions are to be treated under the following heads[1]:

1. Duty to the family;

2. Duty to the immediate community in which we live, and Social Duties;

3. Duty to the State;

4. Duty to Humanity;

5. Duty to self;

6. Duty to things and actions; and

7. Duty to God.

Broad and schematic as this outlined plan necessarily has been, it nevertheless aimed at covering the whole sphere of human duties.

But in revising the constructively ethical part of *Aristodemocracy* it has been strongly impressed upon me that two separate groups of duties, of the utmost importance in the regulation of human conduct, have not been dealt with adequately, or, at least, have not in the general proportion of the scheme received the prominence which is due to them. The first concerns the duty to Truth; the other, what might be called, Sex Morality. Though in several passages (notably on p. 222), the insufficiency of previous ethical systems dealing with Truth has been pointed out, and its importance implied, the crying need for a precise adaptation of the most general commandments against untruth to the modern requirements of a modern code of ethics, and the far greater

[1] *Aristodemocracy, From the Great War back to Moses, Christ and Plato*, London and New York, 1916 and 1917, p. 259.

refinement of the sense of Truth, which our modern civilisation calls for, have not received adequate treatment, and have not had assigned to them the place which, in the proportion of a general scheme of duties, they ought to command. It is the object of this essay to remedy this defect.

As regards Sex Morality, although I have already written the essay on that subject, I have, for cogent reasons, decided to defer publication. I may however be allowed to summarise its leading character and purpose in a few words.

Most of the duties which come under the head of Sex Morality can be, and ought to be, regulated by the several duties as enumerated on p. 259 of *Aristodemocracy* and as developed in the "Outline of the Principles of Contemporary Ethics," Part IV, of that book. The regulation of Sex Morality would specially refer to man's social duties and, still more specially, to the duties of man to woman and woman to man, as well as to man's duty to self. Their consideration would also bear upon his duty to the State and to Humanity.

Furthermore I am strongly convinced that, whatever innovations in the existing ethical laws, as regards sex—both in the married and the unmarried state—may have to be introduced (and these may be numerous and far-reaching), the family, including the home as well as the institution of marriage, will have to be preserved and even strengthened in its hold on society. For I maintain that the family and the home are social units of essential importance to the maintenance of civilised and progressive society. Marriage, the Family and the Home are the *irreducible* units of organised society. However much in the future the evolution and progression of the social and political organisation of social units may remove the conventional barriers of the past and widen out and intensify the relationships of man independently of consanguinity, the family will still remain of the utmost importance and value, and the home can never be dispensed with, in spite of the trend of modern life to overcome all limitations imposed by geographical, local and physical conditions.

To the same degree, I am convinced, must and will the institution of marriage remain in its essential features, though modified, as it will also be strengthened by these modifications. Voltaire's words, "that if God did not exist we should have to invent Him," most fully apply to the institution of marriage. The destructive wave of criticism, which, from the middle of the nineteenth century to our own days, has battered against this stronghold of organised society, has not been able to weaken its foundations or to destroy the essential benefit which it confers upon civilisation. It has shaken, and may carry away, some of the more antiquated conventional outbuildings which have obscured the artistic beauty of the main edifice as well as its capacity for affording security and comfort to men and women; but it has left the central building all the stronger and more beautiful.

No doubt still greater and more radical innovations in our ethical system will have to be introduced for the regulation of Sex Morality of men and women in the unmarried state. Here the problems are as numerous and as complicated as they are pressing in their demands for solution.

Many who in the past have dealt with marriage and the sex relation among the unmarried and many who are dealing with these vital problems now are men and women of un-doubted moral and intellectual sincerity, while some of them are to no small degree representative of higher philosophic thought. But, in most, if not in all, these "revolutionary" writers, I find two blots upon the escutcheon of veracity, or at least two methods of attack which rob their warfare of lasting victory and effectiveness. The first is a danger, to which unconsciously so many of these writers succumb, springing from the ever pervasive personal equation to which even the most thoughtful and self-detached are prone. The peculiar form it takes is that of finding justification or condonation for the satisfaction of their own personal desires in the form of philosophic generalisation, which claims to be—and on the face of it appears to be— emphatically impersonal. Even a Tolstoy regarded these fundamental factors of life very differently in the days of his ebullient and passionate youth when he wrote *Anna Karenina*, *Katia* and other masterpieces, and in the days when vitality was diminished by age and when he wrote *The Kreutzer Sonata* and his religiously moral essays.

A further disqualification which, rightly or wrongly, I can trace in most of these "revolutionary" writers, even—and perhaps especially—in the pure philosophers, is the patent absence of any claim to the widest and most searching experience of life itself in all stratifications of human society and groupings of individuals. I mean the kind of experience such as, for instance, a practising physician, who at the same time is an acute philosopher and a versatile and sympathetic man of the world, might possess—one who has not only received the most complete and intimate confidence from his young and unmarried patients, besides being fully familiar with the social irregularities and misfortunes of the lower strata of society and its outcasts, but who has also had opportunities, within all the unfavourable outcrops of married life, to familiarise himself with all that marriage

really means in the normal life of the home or in the minis-
trations by the sick-bed and the awful solemnity of the hour
of death. Were most of the writers, who would lightly
sweep aside all the traditions that have grouped round the
Sex Morality of the past, possessed of such experience, I venture to doubt whether they would cast out upon the world
the crude theories with which their writings abound.

PART I.

TRUTH IN THE LIFE OF THE INDIVIDUAL

CHAPTER I.

TRUTH AS A NATIONAL TRADITION

"*Dites donc, maman! En Angleterre c'est bien chic de dire la vérité.*" ("I say, mother! In England it is quite the thing [or 'very good form' or 'smart'] to tell the truth.") This remark was made by the young scion of a distinguished French house upon returning to his home after his first term at one of the great public schools of England. There can be no doubt that this testimony to England's moral tone, spontaneously made by a boy, is highly flattering to the English nation and is highly significant in the light it throws both on practical ethics and national psychology. It may, on the one hand, indirectly imply, and bear some testimony to, our national deficiency in manners, our proneness to positive rudeness, and our disregard of other people's feelings, even among those who by tradition and circumstance are the leaders of fashion and strike the keynote of tone in the social life of a country. On the other hand, however, it undoubtedly is a testimony to the prevalence of a sense and a practice of truth throughout all layers of society. A nation, which as a nation, has recognised truth, not only as a moral duty, but has made its practice highly fashionable[1], has

[1] Cf. *Aristodemocracy*, etc., pp. 311 and 312; Appendix VI. pp. 421 and 422.

thereby not only repudiated untruth in its manifest and gross form as a vice, but has effectively stamped even the lighter forms of transgression, which may not always be devoid of social grace, with the brand of ugliness, repulsiveness and vulgarity. The facts with regard to national character and life thus indicated by a casual statement of a child, permeate to the very depths of national consciousness and direct national life as a whole. I venture to say that the England of which the French boy made that sweeping statement could not possibly have a Dreyfus case. By this I do not mean that there could not be found many individuals and groups of people in England who, in the blindness of their personal or partisan passion or even with forethought and "malice prepense," would not have hurled unfounded accusations against an English Dreyfus, and, having made them, would not use every device to maintain their assertions even against their better convictions. But I cannot believe that larger, fully-established and organised national bodies, such as the Army and Navy, political parties, the organisation of definite religious creeds or whole social classes, with the active sanction and connivance of the Government, would have conspired together to block the way to normal legal procedure, and have used every device to bring about a miscarriage of justice. Not only would the national sense of fair-play have been actively potent to a degree which would have made such an episode impossible; but the general abhorrence of the lie, of untruth in any form, for whatever motive, are with us too powerful a factor in public life to have tolerated such proceedings in any of its phases. Still, we must always remember that truth was in the end victorious in France, as indeed no one could doubt that it must eventually be victorious in that great country.

Moreover, no other country in the world could have produced individuals with such undaunted courage and passionate fervour of diction, as was the case with Zola in his famous indictment "*J'accuse.*" It recalled the incident in French history of a century before when Voltaire, the greatest of cynics, stood up against the ruling powers in his noble defence of Calas. Still less could any nation surpass France in producing so glorious a type of its courageous chivalry in the officer who stood firm in the face of the opposition and the menace of his own superiors, of the animosity of his own class, and even of his own traditional personal prejudices, "*sans peur et sans reproche*," as did Colonel Picquart. He was a true and representative son of France.

Not a Question of Race, but of Tradition. It is not a question of race-heredity, nor one of the comparative individual moral value of Frenchmen and Englishmen which makes truth the more potent factor in the actual life of the people in the one country or in the other; but a question of moral education, individual and social, which establishes a general tradition and atmosphere, dominating public as well as private life, and culminating in a ruling passion which, often imperceptibly and unassertively, stamps the life of each country. This tradition and its atmosphere are capable of being fixed, sustained, developed, modified, weakened or strengthened in any given direction by national education in the widest and deepest acceptation of that term. The religious and political martyrs, the heretics and witches who were burnt not so very long ago in England and even in the New England of the Puritan truth-seekers, must give us pause when we arrogate to ourselves the exceptional qualities of truthfulness and justice which distinguish our national life as a differentiating characteristic of the Anglo-Saxon race.

Still the fact remains that with us it is "*chic de dire la vérité*" and that, not only is the confirmed liar despised by us, perhaps even to a greater degree than he is elsewhere, but that we do not like or admire the man or the woman who owe their good manners and their agreeable address to habitual, though minute, sacrifices of veracity in word and in deed. The humbug is as unpopular with us as is the untrustworthy person, or the man who is unbusinesslike in his business affairs.

In spite of National Truthfulness it ranks comparatively low among Virtues. If thus we can claim that as a nation we stand highest in the comparative scale as regards our love and our practice of Truth, close inspection shows us that our own standard, when measured by our clearest and highest conception of what Truth means, and what in practice it ought to mean, in the lives of individuals and of nations—in short, the proportionate weight, which in the whole ethical scale of diverse duties, we assign to Truth—is comparatively low. It looks as if, in the progress of ethical development, following the social evolution of civilised communities, this special duty had lagged behind; so that even those who are most keenly alive and sensitive to the other duties of civilised morality, have a coarser and less developed conception of this group of duties and of the whole weight and bearing of Truth. They have remained satisfied with a rough and rudimentary apprehension of its nature and its dictates. Above all, they have not applied the infinite diversity and refinement, which the scientific and intellectual achievements of centuries of human effort have given to the theoretical endowment of the age to be applied in practice to the prevalent rules of conduct in our everyday life. The result is that members of our communities in every class of

life, whose morality in thought and in conduct in other
spheres is comparatively high, exhibit in their lives, taken
as a whole, a low conception of what Truth really is and
means, and in their daily practice, are guilty of sins of commission and of omission in this one cardinal duty, often
without being aware of the lowness of their moral standards
and conduct. As a natural consequence the general tradition
and the public practice of society as a whole fall woefully
short of the standards which our best thought should enable
us to establish.

I repeat: On the whole the lie is condemned and truth
highly prized among us, we do not cynically admit that it is
right to lie.

Effect of the War on Truthfulness in Public Life. One of the many evils of this war, certainly
not the least, is that the public consciousness
among the belligerents and all over the civilised
world has been impressed with the doctrine
that in war deception by direct untruth is
justifiable. This does not apply only to *ruses de guerre*; but
to the solemn assertions of the leading statesmen, often
made with considerable unction and under the cloak of high
national and humanitarian ideals; to the official and un-
official press; to the practice of the censorship, and to almost
every profession of motive meant to deceive the outer world.
If the records of our own statesmen may be considered
singularly free from the direct sin of commission, I doubt
whether this can be said concerning the numerous sins of
omission which are directly meant to deceive. The com-
motion on the surface of our public life during this war which
has thus stirred up the dregs of lower traditions of public
morality will persist for a long period after the war until the
stream of public life can flow on in unruffled limpidity.

Even before this, however, the prevailing traditions of diplomacy; of our Intelligence Departments with their Secret Service; of our twists and tricks of party manipulation—all had in our public life considerably lowered our standards of Truth from the highest conceptions of our true convictions.

In Private Life.   When we turn to private life the direct or indirect demoralising influence of the war in this special domain of ethics becomes clearly manifest with every day; levity of unconscionable statement is only equalled by uncritical credulity, especially when it means the defamation of character of those prominent in the public eye or even of our immediate neighbours. From the humorous and comparatively harmless myth of the Russians who were landing on our shores (who must undoubtedly have passed through Scotland because the snow was seen on their boots while they were packed in Scottish railway carriages), there have been and will be found people in every walk of life, even some of eminence and distinction, who furnish a whole budget of news ruinously defamatory of the character of their neighbours. The number of prominent people who were reported to have been incarcerated or even executed in the Tower is only surpassed by those who are actually traitors themselves or who have wives or close relations in the pay of the enemy. In every district of the kingdom, rural or metropolitan, grave doubts have been expressed, often leading to cruel persecution, as to the integrity and loyalty of law-abiding citizens; while in many cases, if not in most, the motives of such persecution on the part of those who originated the rumour have not been entirely free from personal interest and jealousy, or in its mildest form, from the survival of *ante-bellum* party antagonism. On the other hand, many a culprit in what in reality is a heinous crime most disastrous in its consequences to the peace and happiness of his neighbours, was not actuated by any such personal motives and may otherwise have possessed most of the other civic virtues as well as chivalry. They merely manifest a gross deficiency in their sense of veracity and in the due appreciation of our supreme responsibility to our neighbours and to ourselves as regards truthfulness of statement and even of inner conviction.

Though the conditions of such a world-upheaval in every direction in public and private life account for the intensification and aggravation of every failing to which human flesh is heir, and directly and physically affect the nerve-balance, judgment and self-restraint of the whole population, and must therefore be regarded with some leniency, the fact remains that these moral failings existed before the war in times of peace.

Comparatively low Standards in Time of Peace. In every class, in every social layer, in every occupation of our common life, we must be struck by the comparative lowness of our moral standards as regards Truth. A village doctor of many years of extended practice throughout a rural district, which, on the whole, stands comparatively high in the morality of its life, confirms my own experience from his wider range of observation. He has found that, though there is but little actual and active dishonesty, theft, or anything approaching to it, in the district, though there also exist considerable helpfulness and kindliness, the bump of Truth among the mass of the population is often represented by a cavity. There is prevalent the grossest bluntness and insensibility in this domain; and the credulity with which the wildest statements are received and transmitted hardly appeals to the sense of humour and rarely evokes resentment when even in a short period they have been shown to be absolutely unfounded. The same applies to many of the ordinary business transactions; and though, as I have said above, direct theft is unknown, unfairness in dealing and even trifling pilfering are common, especially when the marked difference in wealth between the affluent and the poor seems to condone the offence. The only means of combating effectively such crimes destructive of peace and goodwill in village communities, especially among the male population, must be introduced through the medium of the sense of fair-play as a direct result of our national sports and pastimes. The directness and power with which these traditions act are most remarkable and, as I have endeavoured to show elsewhere[1], are a distinctive moral asset of the English-speaking peoples.

If this is the case with our rural population, it applies, if anything, to a greater degree to the traditions of our trade, from the small shopkeeper to the highest financier. Most discouraging of all, however, is the fact that, in what are called the "upper classes," whose opportunities for moral education are of the best, the development of the sense of truth and the duties which it imposes is comparatively most rudimentary. People who would never dream of telling a direct lie to further their own interest or to escape from reproval or responsibility, have no hesitation in light-heartedly contributing to what may take the form of gross slander, to disseminate and actively to confirm its nefarious influence, or, at least, to support by the approval of silence, such a statement made by others when their definite know-

[1] Cf. *What Germany is Fighting for*, III. pp. 93 seq.; and *Nineteenth Century and After*, Dec. 1916.

ledge would enable them to contradict it or when they have at least good reason for doubting its accuracy. Still less prevalent and less admitted and recognised is the responsibility, which every definite statement brings with it, of verifying its accuracy or, at least, of qualifying its absoluteness by an admission of the possibility of doubt. Still rarer, finally, is the individual who fully realises that he has no right to conviction unless it is based upon complete evidence and adequate knowledge.

I am well aware that, with an abnormal growth and with a constant and untimely obtrusion of conscientiousness of statement, even in the lightest matters of daily intercourse and conversation, we should come to the universal development of the "prig," to the destruction of all ease and grace of intercourse and conversation, and to a most dangerous inhibition of intellectual and practical activity in the ordinary flow of our daily existence. Such an objection to the cause I am here pleading would be unfair. The free flow of conversation and of ordinary activity in life would in no way be impeded or diverted by the development and refinement of the sense of truth. On the contrary, as the essence of truth is proportion, and as its apprehension depends upon the weighing of evidence and the nicety of touch in sorting and in distinguishing between the relevant and irrelevant, the possession of this sense to the highest degree in no way robs us of freedom in conversation and intercourse or blunts our lightness of touch in dealing even with the delicacies and intricacies of life. To leave the abstract and impersonal, and to venture upon a personal experience in lieu of argument, I venture to maintain that, in my own past experience, I have known no man possessed of a keener sense of humour and a more graceful appreciation of conversation and of social amenities, than was one of the most accurate and painstaking truth-seekers, one of the foremost philosophers of England, Henry Sidgwick. It will always be just as easy, and infinitely more persuasive, to qualify or modify a statement by whatever light and shade of doubt we may actually feel, than by making an absolute apodeictic statement which implies searching investigation and complete conviction, and, moreover, impresses a finality brooking no contradiction and making an end of all further conversation. But surely I need not further insist upon the evil consequences of misleading statements with regard to facts or misjudgments regarding the actions and motives of other people, leading to error, and giving force and vitality to slander and calumny, which are at the root of much of the unhappiness in the lives of so many people. Nor need I further impress the harm which is done to the mind and to the heart, to the very soul of every person who lowers his own moral dignity by encouraging untruthfulness and coarsening the fibre of his character in the very core of its vitality.

CHAPTER II.

NATIONAL EDUCATION IN TRUTH

Now, the fact remains that in our ethical education, this most important side of our moral life is neglected.

Defective Treatment in Modern Education. Of course I do not mean that in educational systems or practice manifest untruthfulness—lying—is in any way encouraged nor that the injunction "Thou shalt not lie" is not clearly impressed upon the young and implied in the intercourse among adults. But our conception of truth is generally rudimentary and has not kept pace with the evolution of thought and life in the course of centuries of civilised exist- ence. Its conception, adequate to the spirit and achievement of our age, has not been formulated clearly, so as to be grasped even by those who are responsible for the education of the young and who are the public leaders of the nation. Even if it had been formulated and perceived by these, its recognition and its application to actual life have never been directly taught and systematically instilled into the moral training of the young or into the moral and social traditions of adult society. As it has been one of the main purposes of my book *Aristodemocracy* to establish the need of the new codification of modern ethics in general and of insisting upon the necessity of effective teaching of adequate ethics in all civilised communities, so I wish to demonstrate in this essay the special need for the thorough revision of an ethical con- ception of truth and to suggest the efficient means for realising such a conception in the thought and life of future communities.

Practical and Theoretical Aspects of Truth. There are two main aspects of the subject: the theoretical and the practical conception of Truth. As this distinction applies more or less to all other subjects, so also does the fact that it may serve most useful purposes, the two aspects are not separate or opposed to one another, but, on the contrary, interact upon one another and depend for the completeness of their apprehension upon the correct and adequate understanding of each. Any exposition of the practical conception of truth, its application by man to the facts and needs of nature, of life and thought, must depend for its correctness upon the conception which we form of truth itself, as we apprehend it to the best of our cognitive ability. On the other hand, its value for us as human beings is tested by its application to our life and thought, and we are bound to reconsider first principles in the light of our actual experience. A study of man's history in the past throughout the ages has forced upon us the recognition of the changes in the conception of Truth as established by the various forms and systems of philosophy, science or religion which ultimately dominated the actions of those living in these several ages. It can hardly be an over-generalisation to say, that the ethical judgment of each age as a whole depends in great measure, if not wholly, upon the degree in which its life and activity approximated to, or harmonised with, its supreme conception of Truth in the highest manifestation of its thought and religion. We are also justified in maintaining that such an age was either healthy or diseased in the degree in which it lived up to these higher conceptions or ideals of conduct and truth.

CHAPTER III.

THEORETICAL TRUTH

FROM this point of view alone it becomes the duty of the leaders of thought and morality to establish clearly in its purest and highest form the collective conception of Truth which each age has evolved.

"Science." Now it has been one of the shibboleths, constantly proclaimed in and out of place in our own time, that ours is the Age of Science; and it has been assumed that this summary designation will in the future be adopted as essentially defining our own age in the history of thought.

No doubt there has been in the minds of those who make such a generalisation the differentiation of our age from others which may have been called the Ages of Action, of Religion, of Art, etc. Moreover, in accepting such a generalisation, we at once stumble into the main pitfall of obscurity and ambiguity produced by the several conceptions of the term Science: whether it means systematised human knowledge and philosophy, the Greek ἐπιστήμη, or the German "*Wissenschaft*," or whether it means that misleading current denotation of the term in English as synonymous with the natural and exact sciences as distinguished from the humanities, or purely the experimental and mechanical sciences which have made such marked advance in our times and have monopolised so largely the attention of the thinking and unthinking public. Generally, when the term is used on public platforms, not only by ignorant demagogues but even

by distinguished votaries of Science, it means especially the
chemical and mechanical sciences, perhaps including medical
science with those ancillary portions of the natural sciences,
chemical and physical, which minister to its advance in
definite discoveries of therapeutic treatment. Even if other
aspects of scientific investigation (sometimes even graciously
including a slight recognition of the humanities) are not
entirely ignored, the relative importance of these sections of
physical and mechanical sciences is habitually exaggerated.
It is, for instance, interesting to note that so bold, and in-
genious as well as deeply searching, a thinker as is Mr Wells,
reconstructs in his *Anticipations* the whole future of mankind, the classification and gradation of human society and
the personal, ethical, moral and intellectual modification of
the men and women who will constitute it, on the basis of
the decisive achievement of what must be called the
mechanical sciences alone, and he anticipates that they
have, and will have, some influence on the direction which
the social evolution of the future will take, and even on the
mentality of future individual men. This may be admitted.
He even bases the division of social classes on the relative
achievements in this one group of human activities. But
the degree in which the mechanical achievements will regulate social life is ludicrously exaggerated in the generalisations of all these imaginative or unimaginative speculators.
In lieu of an elaborate refutation of such views, in which
innumerable weighty facts bearing upon the main question
might be adduced, I will content myself with merely throwing out, as a suggestion to further thought, one simple and
striking instance from past history, which I am sure these
thinkers will themselves be enabled, by the rapid receptivity of their fertile and intensely active brains, to apply to

the present question and to appreciate as a weighty argument against their main generalisation. There can be no doubt that the invention of gunpowder in 1330 contributed materially to the downfall of feudalism. But throughout the succeeding ages, smaller and larger communities and the civilised world at large have still been practically ruled by certain governing people who have not been dependent for their dominating influence and power as individuals or as classes upon their own direct share in the invention or application of such mechanical forces. In England, one of the most democratic of all countries, we still have a House of Lords, and neither here nor in other countries are the great inventors themselves possessed of the guiding or directing abilities to act as leaders in the social and political life of the nation.

Nevertheless the generalisation that ours is the Age of Science, and, moreover, that the inductive and experimental sciences have powerfully modified the consciousness of the second half of the nineteenth century, as they do of our own age, is undeniable.

Deduction and Induction. No doubt we must recognise and value the contribution to Truth made by the deductive methods of logic and metaphysic, and of theological study, as well as of pure mathematics and those departments of applied science which come under its sway. But the achievement of the great experimenters and thinkers of the nineteenth century, among whom Darwin must be placed at the head, has, in the light of the present inquiry, established one supreme fact, both in its negative and in its positive aspect, which has essentially modified our whole thought and our conception of Truth. We admit and we can fully appreciate the pursuit of the purely deductive

sciences and the justification and trustworthiness of their
results in themselves, as pure logic and abstract sciences,
but we have made the important—nay the essential—discovery, that where they are not trustworthy, and where
error and all the fatal consequences attendant upon error
may creep in, is in the *application* of these deductive principles to the organic world and especially to life—to man's
relation to man and human society, to the spiritual life and
its complexities. In plain words this means: that Truth does
not come by inspiration, but by experience; that, however
perfect the brain it cannot, of itself, discover and establish
Truth; but that, for the understanding of life and nature, it
must work on accurate observations and experience (in some
cases even experiment) before Truth is attained. So-called
intuition and introspection are not enough. For (at least
in adult life) these deal with the material of innumerable
unconscious or subconscious experiences, transmitted to
some degree by heredity, but chiefly by outer stimuli and
data accumulated at haphazard, without any method or
accuracy, and, often, if not generally, forming a solid mass
of prejudice and even superstition. It is in this *application*
of brain power to experience that we find, in looking at the
past, that mankind has gone wrong, and that it is likely to
go wrong in the future; that in this sense truth and untruth
depend upon the application which is made of our deductive
faculties.

So much for the negative aspect of our discovery. The
positive aspect (firmly established and fixed in our mentality
by the great achievements of the scientific investigators and
philosophers grouping, as equal luminaries or as minor
satellites, round the central constellation of Darwin) has
established and enthroned, as the ruling power in the dis-

covery of Truth, the empirical and inductive methods which are the final tests of its validity, even though the truth may be the same as that discovered by the deductive method of thought, which the modern empiricist is growing more and more to respect and to value. They are, as a matter of fact, correlative forces in the establishment of Truth. Nay, even further than this,—the more soberly and conscientiously, and with the supreme exertion of intellectual will-power, the truth-seeker curbs the impulses of personal desire and passion, of imagination and of intellectual and logical formalism, which constitute the Beauty of Pure Thought, the more is he able to appreciate and to value the synthetic function and power of the imagination—of art—and the more is he capable of realising all the demands of conscious human life in its effort towards progress and in its establishment of the highest ethical laws. But the intellectual morality born of this inductive and empirical discipline in the study of nature and of man,—of man's life and thought as well,—is opposed to all generalisation which merely depends upon imagination, intuition, or even upon logical deduction. It only admits a generalisation into the sacred precincts of Truth after it has passed through the narrow and laborious avenues of experimental test, of conscientious in duction; after the negative instances have been bravely sought out, faced and overcome. For these negative instances, when overcome, pave the way to legitimate generalisation and fix and confirm the solid dominion of Truth. On the other hand hasty imaginative thought and passionate diction, as well as remote and isolated deduction, dwelling in the attenuated spheres and pure ether where organic life cannot subsist, undermine the very foundations of the fortress of Truth.

Now this conception of Truth, evolved by our own age, has permeated the whole of our national consciousness—our *ethos*—even for those who are far removed from spheres of philosophic thought, who do not even know what such terms as "deduction" and "induction," "experiment" and "generalisation" mean; and even though this conception of Truth be flagrantly disregarded or positively sinned against by many of the leaders of thought, and by most of those who are responsible for the education of the young and for the economical, social and political life of the adult population. Do and say what they will, and though they may turn their backs on the light which illumines the intellectual and moral life of our western civilisation, though its principles, and, especially, its bearings upon our daily life, may be denied, this distinctive conception of Truth has, and will have to a greater degree, a guiding and directing influence upon the morality of our time. In so far, the distinctive quality of our sense of Truth differs from that of by-gone ages. It has begun to modify our lives as well as our thoughts, and it remains with us as the most important duty of every thinker, teacher and leader of men to make its sway more real, effective and universal. Above all, we must boldly advance against those powerful and prominent representatives of thought who, generally misguided by enthusiasm, prejudice, or the passionate impulse of artistic exaggeration, raise the standard of one-sided fanaticism, and thus betray their allegiance to the stern-eyed goddess of Truth.

I have endeavoured to illustrate the practical and ethical bearings of this conception of Truth in contrasting the influence which the dangerous habits of mind of two great men, Carlyle and Ruskin (possessing the *défauts de leurs qualités*), had in the past with that of the truth-loving leader of thought, Charles Darwin, the eager guide to the practical ethics of Truth in modern life[1]:

In the case of Ruskin, and in the case of his master in some departments, Carlyle, the prevalence of the relentless, exaggerated, denunciatory frame of mind and form of expression has often beguiled them away from the noble course of sober and conscientious search after truth, absorbing much of the energies that are painfully needed to reduce to order the tangled web of the innumerable facts that crowd round the narrow gateways of conclusions justified by truth. It has kept them from curbing subjective impulses, strong desires and passions and prejudices, and of bending their energies to the service of the stern-browed goddess; it has lured them on to the riotous chase of the maenad whom they mistake for a muse. The prophetic denunciatory tone in its resounding flow may prove to be an easy means of shirking and avoiding the great task of declaring to men the hard-won truths that are announced in simple, diffident, nay, halting words, but still penetrate and endure in their far-reaching quality of sound. And ultimately the result upon such men themselves, and a baneful influence upon all who come within the circle of their power, is a general blunting of the keen edge of what we must call intellectual morality, that moral and mental habit which makes it impossible for any man to state as an undoubted fact whatever he has not conscientiously tested and examined in all its bearings.

There is nothing we would plead for more earnestly than moderation in matters intellectual. We are often told that exaggeration is demanded to reach and move the masses, in order that a general truth might become practically effectual and leave the spheres of pure thought. We are informed that minute and careful balancing of truth finds its place in the silent study; but that, when we go out into the market-place and thoroughfares of actual life, we need direct and forcible

---

[1] See *The Work of John Ruskin*, by the present writer, Methuen & Co., London and New York, Harper & Brothers, 1893, pp. 168 seq.

statements, figures of prophets and movers of men who stand out strongly as types of the one idea which they incorporate— comparative coarseness of intellectual fibre and passionate boldness of expression. Luther moved men, we are told, not Melanchthon and the humanists. It has almost become a commonplace to say: not the sober student, but the prophetic enthusiast is required to effect great changes in the world's history. I will not attempt here to answer the question whether, if we look into history carefully, we shall not find that, after all, the moderate student was not more efficient in turning the world's current into lasting and beneficent channels than the violent enthusiast, and that the latter really only became influential when he made himself the mouthpiece of the former. I should further suggest the question whether each exaggerated movement does not bring with it a corresponding reaction, corresponding in strength to the degree of exaggeration, and acting, in the long-run, as a retarding force to human progress, quite out of proportion to any temporary gain apparent at the time of the exaggeration? If we must needs have strong preaching, then there is one topic for the moralist and world-reformer in which exaggeration is least likely to be harmful—the gospel of Sanity and Moderation.

Ruskin has often allowed his feelings to run counter to the workings and injunctions of this higher duty. In the preface to the *Seven Lamps* there are " cases in which men feel too keenly to be silent, and perhaps too strongly to be wrong": he ought to have guarded most jealously against the strong feelings as often making it more probable that we may go wrong. The use of superlative adjectives condemning or praising, with him and with Carlyle, points to the same bluntness of intellectual morality. One thing or work is wholly " bad," another at once all that is " good." He passes judgment not only upon all forms of art, but upon the works of great and sober men of science, on the problems of these departments of science themselves, whether it be the works of an Agassiz or of a Darwin, the purport of whose work he had never trained himself to realise. Such exaggerations may, alas, from a literary point of view appear to be innocent, but in their effect they certainly are not.

He will, for instance, in *Praeterita*, II, page 298, tell us, with the emphatic terms of a convinced authority, speaking of Sydney Smith's *Elementary Sketches on Moral Philosophy*, that "they contain in the simplest terms every final truth which any rational mortal needs to learn on this subject." We must ask what right his reading of that vast subject called philosophy has given him to pass judgment in any way upon it. And so, in almost every chapter of all his books, we cannot help feeling that this is a positive blemish, the influence of which cannot be good; and we turn with pure gratitude to his descriptive passages, where there is no scope for this intellectual vice, and where the good that is in him has brought forth fruit that will be the delight and profit of all the ages in which the English language is read. If, as far as intellectual example is concerned, we turn from the prophetic and denunciatory violence of Carlyle and Ruskin to the charitable and unselfish statement of a great continuous effort in a long laborious life, beautiful as it is simple, we cannot help feeling that, besides the results of the actual research of Charles Darwin, his literary and scientific example as a writer can but have a lasting and elevating influence upon the minds of all those who read him for generations to come. No amount of denunciatory sermons can replace the unconscious preaching contained within the work and its results of the student who has honestly mastered a subject, however narrow its range. This is the highest form of preaching, if only for the supreme effect, the suppression of impulse and passion for an end that has no immediate bearing upon our own interests, and does not flatter our vanity in the elevation of our own position to that of a direct teacher or chastiser of foolish humanity, and above all in the jealous custody and possible refinement of our feeling for truth[1]. It appears to me one of

[1] "The development of this intellectual morality as a habit in individuals, and as a tradition in a nation and in an age, is intimately connected with practical morality and truthfulness; and there appears to me to be a strong moral and disciplinary bearing in the methods of research as applied to the natural sciences within our days, to which Charles Darwin has chiefly contributed. It is true, the inductive method was recommended by Bacon and insisted upon by Hume;

the greatest blemishes in the work of men like Ruskin and Carlyle that, however high the position they may themselves assign to truth in their moral scales, the actual tenor of their work has counteracted rather than favoured this desirable consummation. Bearing this in mind, we can recognise the good that is in Ruskin's work, and there will be enough of merit remaining to make him one of the great benefactors of mankind.

I wish above all that the main point which I have attempted to illustrate in these references to Charles Darwin be not misunderstood. The influence of Darwin on his generation and ours, upon which I am here insisting, is not that specifically exerted by his Theory of Evolution as the basis for a Philosophy of Nature and Human Life and Thought—as a *Weltanschauung*—powerful as no doubt his work has been in our times, or perhaps for all times, in affecting the Natural Sciences and in producing in Humanistic Studies the historical or genetic methods in opposition to the mere recording of facts in nature and their classification, or the more static conception of man's actions and thoughts in the past and the present. In the Copernican era of thought such discoveries exerted the most powerful influence on the Time Spirit, but became modified by succeeding discoveries or even superseded by a new Time Spirit. So Weissmann's researches and criticisms, the school of Biology identified with the name of Mendel and other thinkers and students may have modified the original Darwinian Theory of Evolution, until it may be superseded

but it has only become a fact in Darwin; and through his efforts and those of his numerous followers and co-operators the general habit of mind which is developed by their methods of work has not only penetrated into other regions of thought and study, but it is modifying and raising our general standard of truth even in our practical daily life."

by a new conception of Natural Philosophy—a new *Weltan-schauung*. My introduction of the work of Charles Darwin here used in illustration is not concerned with this aspect of his theory and achievement, but wholly with his *method of work*,—with the process of experiment, induction and thought through which he arrived at his generalisation. The result of this method is here applied directly to the *ethics* of thought and life. As such it remains, and will ever remain, nobly efficient as a stepping-stone and guide to the attainment of immediate and ultimate Truth.

CHAPTER IV.

PRACTICAL TRUTH

THE supreme importance of instilling into the youthful mind the adequate modern conception of theoretical Truth will be admitted by those who are responsible for the education of the young, as it will also be realised by the adult that he must religiously cultivate and refine this conception in himself. We must thus first consider Inner Truth, i.e. Truth in its relation to ourselves, and then proceed to examine it in its relations to outer nature and the world of things; and finally in its bearings upon our relation to our fellow-men, the social aspect, both in deed and word. To put it epigrammatically: Truth in its relation to ourselves produces mental Honesty; to nature and the world of things, Efficiency; and in its social relation, in controlling our actions towards our fellow-men, Justice and Charity, as in our word it produces Trustworthiness and Honour.

CHAPTER V.

HONESTY

NOT only in the form of moral feeling of a general character, but by direct intellectual precept and practice must we keep this distinctive nature of theoretical Truth untarnished within us and not defile it either by direct contravention or by compromise. We must be neither hypocrites nor humbugs; neither deceivers of others nor of ourselves. Our convictions must be reasonably established, not hastily constructed on hearsay or guesswork, nor undermined by personal desires and by prejudice.

Artistic Truth, Imagination. In forming our convictions we must mistrust not only our desires and passions, but our imagination and our artistic sense, which so often lead our thoughts to run riot, while in a milder manifestation, they at least confirm a tendency to sacrifice truth and accuracy to harmony and symmetry of form, and produce an intellectual leniency which is so well expressed in the French phrase "*Enjoliver n'est pas mentir.*" But this restriction in no way denies the rights and the claims of imagination, the charm of the unexpected and even of the fantastic, which are the humour of intellect. These faculties have established their supreme spiritual right in the healthy development of the human mind, as in the civilised life of man Art is the correlative of Science. Nor need we deny the moral and artistic quality of mystery and mysticism, of romance and of all the pure productions of the imagination. There is truth in imaginative creation, truth even in the grotesque: they present the contrast to the normal, the recreative relief from the dominance of sterner intellectual duty. In so far, they are not only admissible, but useful in their function: they stimulate and re-invigorate the faculty of reason and morality—provided always they do not defile the purity of the intellect by intrusion into its own domain and by snatching its sceptre or by assuming its garb.

Mystery and Romance. True mystery and mysticism are not to be found in the revelry of savage imagination, but in the idealism of the trained and cultivated intellect. Nature provides mystery and mysticism enough in its myriad objects; in their origin, growth, decay or resurrection; and man's spirit, in the purest and highest form of its intellectual development, contains motives enough which lead and strive towards infinity along the paths of reason and truth (which themselves lead to the highest and remotest ideals), to respond to the love of mystery and mysticism, without bowing to the worship of the irrational. The worship of Athene is higher than that of the Maenad; savage man established the latter, civilised man, through countless ages of intellectual effort and refinement and through the devoted life-blood of thinkers and martyrs, has established the former. Though in our sane moments we all admit the sovereignty of the clear-eyed goddess, the survival of the savage or the beast in us leads us to disown our allegiance to her at the slightest call of the raving Maenad, who drags us in wild chase through the woods and forests of primeval man, as she also glides through the slums of the cities and the gilded palaces of the rich and mighty. We then wish to escape from the rule of reason, though in doing so we deny our own self and the best that is in us; and by elaborate sophistry, fixed in tradition, we often successfully endeavour to make ourselves believe that there is virtue in such apostasy.

Admiration and Wonder. If admiration is one of the highest qualities of the heart and mind, wonder is one of the lowest. Yet so strong is this primeval instinct towards change and life in the senses of man, that he is constantly straining after the new thing, the uncommon thing, the irrational thing, and the physical justification of this elementary impulse of vitality is so strong that it will often attack and overbear the reasonableness and truthfulness of the most highly trained and refined intelligence.

The Quack-Doctor. All the results of patient and conscientious medical study developed through centuries of mental effort will be cast to the winds with the beating of the drum and the ringing of the bells of the quack in the market-place and the savage who has thus re-awakened in civilised man exults and revels in the defection of kindly Minerva (whom, as a civilised man, he had patiently followed, and whom in this surviving savage heart of his, he hates), in order to follow the Maenad of barbarism and imposture.

The Young Mind. Though it may be right and wise in due proportion directly to cultivate and develop the imagination in the young by encouraging games of "pretence," by reading fairy tales and by romance, it must never be done at the cost of weakening and coarsening the sense of Truth; and though the religious emotions, in lifting the child's mind above the sensual materialism of its daily impressions towards the spiritual striving of an ideal world, may be good and necessary, it cannot be good to instil into the core of its mental constitution the disturbing and unbalancing forces of the irrational in any one of the forms of religious dogma. A twist and turn is thereby given to the mind, in the earliest and most helpless phase of its innocent plasticity, from which it may never recover, which may unright the balance of its intellect in the apprehension of Truth for the whole of its life, and, in some cases, may sow the pathological germs developing sooner or later into insanity.

The Adult.   If this be especially the case with the young, it applies to almost the same degree to the mental discipline and self-training of adults. Superstition of apparently the most harmless kind must be discouraged, in fact, must be combated by the continuous exertion of will. We must jealously guard our desires so that they do not intrude into our observation of facts and our thoughts concerning facts, disturb their accuracy and dissolve their truth. Uncommonness and wondrousness in themselves, unless they are justified and strengthened by moral or artistic qualities and thus evoke admiration, must set us on our guard instead of attracting us into ready acceptance. In any case, they must stimulate us to an exceptional effort to test their justification.

Limitation of Knowledge. Acceptance of New Truths.   The man of most highly-trained mind, who has embodied in his mentality all the achievements and results of science, is most modest and most ready to admit the limitations of his own information as well as of the collective knowledge of his age. He has been prepared by experience to realise how, in his own day as well as in by-gone ages, new discoveries, unheard, even undreamt of before, have run counter to the established experiences of the world. He is prepared to accept new and uncommon evidence even when it is subversive of a whole group of truths and a consequent generalisation or even a so-called "law" which would apparently exclude its possibility. But it is not the newness of the discovery as such, still less its subversiveness of established experience and tradition, which attract him or favour reception into his own convictions. It is only after he has been convinced of the truth of the new phenomenon itself and after he has been able to fit it into the whole body of rational consciousness that he is prepared fully to accept it. For this body of rational consciousness has been established in his own mind and in the minds of his fellow-men, not only by the logic of thought, but by the countless experiences of innumerable reasonable beings through ages of transmitted and recorded thought and experience.

Röntgen Rays, Wireless Telegraphy, Psychic Force. To give but two instances; he would thus accept the discovery of the Röntgen Rays, which implies a kind of visual perception through solid bodies, and wireless telegraphy, the most startling "mystery" of modern scientific discovery. It may also—in the future—be the case with the recognition of "psychic thought-waves." But the man of refined scientific truthfulness gratefully and admiringly accepts these new contributions to Truth, even though before their discovery they may have contravened cumulative experience of lawful possibilities, because there is irrefutable evidence in fact, tested and demonstrated by experience, and because, so far from contravening the laws of thought and of logic upon which our sanity is based, they confirm these laws by their rational position in the physical principles which science has established. It is not *in opposition to* the dominant code of scientific Truth that acceptance of such discoveries is claimed and granted, but under the supreme aegis of its guidance and in confirmation of. its rule.

Revolt from Science. But we must always remember that the spirit of independence and licence, arising out of the fundamentally noble passion for liberty, coupled with the natural desire for change and the attraction of newness, is likely to be the primary as well as the ultimate motive power in those self-deceived seekers after Truth who oppose the established laws of evidence and science, and prematurely clamour for the acceptance of theories and discoveries which run counter to the dominant code of evidence and are far from being justified by experience and induction.

The Worshippers of the Commonplace and of the Uncommon. This attraction inherent in new and revolutionary theories may sometimes—though unconsciously—be increased by the flattering consciousness of distinction which comes from standing alone or in the company of a few of the elect against the horde of the undistinguished Worshippers of the Commonplace. Whether these be the effective motives or not, the fact remains that sound and devoted research, which concentrates all energy upon the discovery of new truths in the silent study or the laboratory, is prematurely dragged out into the clamorous market-place, enlists a large body of vociferous coadjutors and adherents, eminently disqualified for conscientious research, often transfusing the scientific body with the passion of partisanship and, in any case, demoralising these unqualified investigators in their own sense of Truth and their intellectual morality and sanity and lowering the aggregate morality of the whole community.

Psychical Research. This applies in some instances—though certainly not in all—to such a body as the Society for Psychical Research. In justification of the existence of such a widely diffused and popular body it may be urged, that it is necessary to enlist the interest and co-operation of the widest possible number of people in order to collect the greatest amount of evidence. But the inclusion of large numbers of active workers eminently unqualified for research is disastrous in its effects in every direction. Such people are in no way qualified to test evidence nor do they possess the methods and habits of scientific investigation. Their co-operation is thus worse than useless, while their concentration on abnormal experiences with which they are unable to deal rationally is most demoralising to their own mentality and their sense of Truth.

The qualities eminently required for such investigation are, in the first instance, those of the psychologist, especially the neuro-psychologist, and, still more especially the neuropathologist, the nerve doctor. To these must be added all the qualities which go to the making of the ideal judge in the weighing of evidence, and the most acute cross-examiner in the testing of it. And, finally, it would require the fusion of these qualities into the sympathetic mentality of the true man of the world, whose varied, if not universal, experience of life, of men and of women and of the human heart, enables him, on the one hand, to enter into the life and thought of every class of people, as, on the other hand, his vast experience of human nature, its motives and habits of thought and action, would protect him against credulity and would constantly put him on his guard against all tricks of untruthfulness and habits of self-deception in others. But, above all, there would be needed in such an ideal investigator the absence of all alien motives—alien to the immediate and exclusive discovery of Truth by observation and the weighing of evidence. Such disturbing motives arise from the passionate desire to seek for confirmation of the most elementary and justified longings of the human heart and mind, such as the desire for personal immortality and the longing for communion with those who have been nearest to our life and heart and whom death has removed from us.

This kind of research would require to a most exceptional degree intellectual self-control and the inductive habit of mind which are prepared constantly to repress and to counteract the allurements of deductive thought. In so far it will be found that, even among men of science, those who have had to deal with organic phenomena or with humanistic studies which are inductive in method—with the problems of life and mind—are better fitted for dealing with such evidence than are mathematicians or those who deal with the inorganic world. The more their methods approach to those of pure mathematicians,—even though these latter are exponents of a sublime realm of thought, unapproachable by the average mind of even the great thinkers in other departments of science—the less are they often fitted to deal with the problems of life and mind.

I venture, however, to say that for the general run of unscientific people and, especially for those who have never been trained in the strict schooling of inductive thought; such active participation in "psychical research" and the dwelling in such regions of attenuated thought, out of all relation to the conscious and subconscious interests of their natural daily life, is most demoralising and destructive of their pure sense of truth, and may in many cases, lead to pathological abnormalities of mind and conduct. To give but one analogy (analogies may always be dangerously inaccurate and misleading) I maintain that the case could be similar, though not identical, if a wide and popularly founded society for Pathological Research were established among us, in which the members, free from every taint of medical training, were invited to send evidence with regard to their own pathological symptoms, to furnish material for the more effective study of diseases, and if all the members took some active part in the collecting of such evidence and the bearings which it has upon final and practical generalisation. Whatever results might thus be attained, one result would, to my mind, be undoubtedly produced; i.e. the increase of hypochondriasis in various forms of hysteria, as the continuous dwelling upon ghost stories and exceptional psychic phenomena may ultimately lead to the definite disease of hallucination in those who, without preparation and qualification, deal with these subtle subjects. But above all I venture to hold that the healthy *moral*, as it is concerned with the sense of truth in the lay members of such pathological or psychological societies, is seriously impaired and lowered.

Superstition. Of course this is still more the case with all habits of gross superstition, and it cannot be urged with too much insistence that a grave responsibility rests upon those who thoughtlessly and lightly instil by slovenly and good-humoured example the poison of the irrational and the untrue in the minds of the young and among those over whom they have some influence—and even in themselves[1].

[1] I may mention that it has been a distressing and disheartening experience to find, that in a gathering of friends of intellectual eminence, while playing Bridge, many will insist upon choosing the line of the hinges in the table, will fuss over the choice of seats, and even perform such capers as turning their chairs round three times when they have a spell of ill-luck. There can be no doubt that bad cards bring bad luck; but no sane man can believe that it is "bad luck" which brings bad cards.

W. T. 3

Honesty

Spook-Habit and Drug-Habit.

Still more distressingly baneful is the wide-spread practice of professional clairvoyants and palmists and "mediums" of all sorts, which is not only affecting the idle, credulous and brainless people, whose unimportant lives are on a level with their low intellectual *moral*, but is also affecting the health, the peace of mind and the efficiency of those who fall under such influence, as much, and in the same manner as does the "drug-habit." Far from infrequently the results of such practices have led to most tragic issues, and the health and happiness of individuals and of whole families have been wrecked; while the frivolous half-approving tolerance with which striking and confirmatory instances are repeated, and even accepted, by those who are far from being victims, produces an aggregate mental tone in society, which effectively, though insidiously, lowers the truthful mentality of a large number of people.

All these evil practices of superstition and imposture may lead to what, in one phrase, may be called the formation of the Spook-Habit. The Spook-Habit and the Drug-Habit are —if not brothers—cousins of the same original stock. As the Drug-Habit undermines our physical health so the Spook-Habit destroys our moral and intellectual health, our balance of mind, our judgment, and our appreciation of truth; while both together disintegrate our whole moral fibre. A neuras-thenic, hyper-emotional or hysterical person in many cases loses the sense of truth and can never be depended upon to do the reasonable, right and just thing. He may be kind, generous, even brave and self-sacrificing; but he may also be unreasonable and unjust, even cruel, mean and cowardly when "upset" or carried away by passion or by delusion— we might sometimes as well trust a madman as one of these.

The Spook-Habit, like the Drug-Habit, generally takes its rise in small beginnings. An illness coupled with pain or *malaise*, a state of nerve tension with worry and distress may be relieved by an "innocuous" dose of some mild drug. The habit is gradually formed and demands ever increasing doses in volume and strength until the man or woman becomes its slave. A superstition of the "most harmless" order ("say rabbit three times and you will receive a present," "the thirteenth chair")[1], the hearing of a ghost-story, or a shock or hallucination, quasi-religious suggestion[2], the constant use of the word *"unberufen"*— out of all these seeds sown in youth, growing insidiously and subconsciously in the young mind, the weeds which

---

[1] It may be apposite to refer here to the play of that title (*The Thirteenth Chair*) which has met with well-merited success, for a play of that order, as I am writing. The imposture in the practices of the clairvoyant are well exposed, and, in so far, the effect of the play is wholesome. But it is to be regretted that in the last effective scene the author has given way and has relinquished his higher standards. That the voice of the murdered man should be heard may be accounted for by ventriloquism as practised by the clairvoyant. On the other hand the door flying open at the critical moment and the murderer's knife dropping from the ceiling, though conceivably due to coincidence, suggest supernatural intervention and in so far confirm the morbid public in their superstitions.

[2] Among many similar proofs of the unbalancing effects upon the child-mind of harmful thoughts and feelings produced in a quasi-religious form, I have heard from a mother, how she was attracted to the cot of her child lying awake in fear and torture and screaming "I do not want to be carried away by the angels," being told that angels carried the dead children to heaven. Child-life is not to be deprived of the brightness and charm which dwell in fairyland, nor is the imagination to be starved. But moral, intellectual and artistic food must be carefully administered to the youthful mind in order not to impair mental health.

overspread the whole fertile field of the mind at last submerge and kill all the healthy plants of a rational and wholesome mentality.

But not only children must be carefully guarded against these evils; our adult population must protect itself and be protected by the State[1], from such disastrous moral diseases which often partake of the character of epidemics. Nations as well as individuals may be ruined by these diseases. It is not overstating the case to say, that the catastrophic collapse of the Russian nation is in great part due to the effect upon the people (lacking as they also do all political as well as general education), of the gross or widespread forms of religious superstitions which permeate and dominate all classes of the population. It is not only the barely civilised Mudjik who is thus ruled and obsessed by superstitions of all kinds. There are "highly-educated" men and women of intellectual vigour and refinement, disciples of Darwin and Herbert Spencer or of modern German materialists, who manifest the most incredible childishness in accepting, and submitting to, superstitions; until at last we come to the tragedy, centring round Rasputin, with his nefarious vogue in the Russian court, gruesomely grotesque in its immoral, terrifically stupid coarseness and depravity, which crowns the last reign of idiocy and superstition and ushers in the lawless, absolutely unbridled sway of Bolshevik

---

[1] The prosecution of all clairvoyants, palmists and similar impostors must be vigorously carried on by the State. Even Hypnotism and Suggestion are not to be practised by unqualified agents. As an *Anesthetician* must be duly qualified before he can practise, so ought those in charge of the important therapeutic department of Hypnotism and Suggestion to be vigorously controlled. As the distribution of poisonous or dangerous drugs is regulated by the State, so should the drugs of the mind be guarded.

"liberty" still governed by the inherited methods of previous corruption and tyranny.

The Right to an Opinion. To leave these morbid—and let us hope—more unusual causes of mental demoralisation, we come to the most widespread and less manifest, though most effective, source of lowered truthful vitality. It concerns the formation and the holding of opinions. There never was a more fatally untrue saying than the statement that "every man has the right to an opinion," and even that "every man has a right to his own opinion." We are here not dealing with expression of opinion only, but even with the holding of it. It is probably nearer the truth to say, "that but few people have a right to an opinion and only have a right to their own opinion when it is justified by experience, thought and all the tests which go to the making of conviction." This is one of the first and cardinal lessons of the ethics of Truth which are to be instilled into the young mind and are to be maintained in their fulness in the convictions and mental habits of adults. When we seriously consider the matter it will be found that it is not at all necessary for us to form an opinion upon a great many subjects, especially when we realise that the means of ascertaining facts and drawing trustworthy conclusions from them, and the capacity and training to deal with such problems, are not given to us. One of the first precepts which should be inculcated in the young is the unequivocal admission, not only to others, but to themselves, "*I don't know.*" The teacher and parent, and all those responsible for the training of young people, must impress this by example and must frankly admit their own limitations and their fallibility. There is no greater error—untrue in itself intellectually and morally as well as impolitic in view of the maintenance of educational authority—than that the maintenance of authority depends upon an estimate of infallibility which the young are to form of their elders, or that the authority is lowered when belief in such infallibility is not absolute. As this applies to the estimate and consequent influence concerning the personality of the teacher, so it ought to be maintained in every department and in every item of actual instruction. The plea that hesitation, qualification and doubt produce uncertainty and confusion in the minds of the learners, is unfounded. No science, no department of instruction, depends upon, or is benefited by, overstatement. While the moral result and the intellectual training, the increase of precision in observation and judgment, the stimulation to mental effort, and finally, the production of an *ethos*. a general character of strong and refined truthfulness, are born from hesitation in judgment and from the admission on the part of the teacher, "I don't know," "I have no right to an opinion on the matter," or "I have, as yet, no right to an opinion." However important it be to teach those deductive subjects (reading, writing, arithmetic, geography, etc.) which form our elementary studies and give a groundwork of fact upon which the reasoning powers are to be employed, it is most important that the inductive subjects, including experiment, should be taught, not so much for their own intrinsic value and practical importance, as for the moral discipline which they induce in every child, whatever its natural bent or the probable future lines of study or work which it will have to pursue in after life. For it is through them that this moral process in the finding and in the justification of conviction is most clearly and effectually impressed upon the child's mind.

The greatest care will also have to be exercised *The Teaching of History.* in the teaching of history. For it is in this department that the truth-seekers have sinned with most disastrously tragic results in the promotion of the "national" spirit which has favoured the violent, unreasoning and savage animosity culminating in this great war. Histories, especially school histories, will have to be re-written all over the world. The aim of history must be the establishment of Truth, not the production of patriotism or any other passion or quality, however desirable and noble. The duties of patriotism may be directly impressed upon the young, with all the justification which they possess; but the study of man's past must be solely guided by the desire to know the truth concerning his past and shall admit of no other motive. As the teaching of history must never be biassed by patriotic or religious prejudice, so must the personal bias of the writer and the teacher be carefully guarded against. In any case, do not let the child go away with a feeling of finality in judgment either of the past periods in history or of the great men of former days. Do not hesitate to qualify judgments and to leave the child in doubt where certainty is not attainable.

I shall deal with the numerous and important cases in which the need of immediate action and the choice of one or other alternative require the formation of an opinion, and the case where probability and preference must take the place of certainty and moral necessity. But where the need of action, the necessity to "take sides," and the duty to express one's opinion *ad hoc*, are not imposed, the right to form an opinion on insufficient data does not exist.

The Honest Man. Finally there remains the summary of all the duties of man in the relation of Truth to himself. "Know thyself" has for ages been recognised as one of the supreme moral duties of man. It implies the necessity for positive self-inquiry. Still more important is the negative aspect of this duty: "Do not deceive thyself. Do not try to make others believe, and thyself believe, that thou art what thou art not." Among the most despicable of human beings are those who live a lie before others; but almost more despicable are those who live a lie to themselves. The realisation of Truth in its relation to ourselves produces the Honest Man. The honest man is essentially the same now as he was in the half-animal existence of the early cave-dwellers. But, as the conditions of life have been infinitely multiplied and varied since the days of these primitive phases in human evolution, so have our powers of thought and our habits of thinking advanced and increased; and the conceptions which we hold of Truth differ, not only from those of primitive man, but even from the man of a century ago, nay, a generation ago; and it is therefore our duty to become conscious of this new conception of Truth, as the expression of the civilisation to which we have attained, and to live up to it.

CHAPTER VI.

EFFICIENCY

WHEN now we leave this inner life and turn to the practical life of the outer world we again find, that upon our adequate conception of Truth and upon the efficient habit with which it has permeated our observation, our understanding and our various activities in dealing with this outer world depend to the greatest degree, even our success or failure in life, in the business of life—our Efficiency. In this business of life man deals with nature and the world of things, but he also deals with his fellow-man in so far as man possesses, produces or modifies these things of the world, co-operates with him in common effort or competes with him in possession or control, in friendly rivalry or unfriendly struggle. Here it is most important that observation and understanding should guide action to a successful issue. Observation, to lead to perfect understanding, should be clear and unbiassed. Action, to be effective, must include the true and just apprehension of the relation of these outer objects to man himself, his capacities and his limitations in dealing with these objects of the outer world.

Practically the bulk of our educational training, all the phases of our schooling and our apprenticeship, are concerned with fitting us for this struggle in the business of life. Skill and dexterity of hand, of our senses and mind, must be whetted and perfected in order to impress man's creative genius, his needs and his desires upon the outer world of things. But, however great his skill in the manipulation of his appropriate tools, in all the technical process of work, success and efficiency above all depend upon their guidance by the human intelligence which has accurately grasped the true nature of the objects thus to be affected, of their receptivity to such work and of man's own power to bend them to his will. Practical and technical capacity is not enough to produce capability in subjugating things of the outer world to man's use. Correct apprehension, reason and judgment, are the guides which enable him to master all the conditions and processes in this technical struggle with the world of affairs. The truer and more perfect this theoretical instrument which guides the technical tool, the more likely is the work of man's hand to be successful. This means, in other words, not only that his faculty for apprehending truth and assimilating it with his own mentality, his conscious and subconscious mind, should be healthy and complete, but, also, that his conception of Truth itself should be of the highest and purest form, adequate to the mental development of his age, and not borrowed from by-gone ages which in so far stood on a lower level of intellectual development and whose standards of Truth are, in consequence. of a lower order.

Now it is owing to the deficient apprehension and practice on this side of education and self-culture that result all those incompetencies and inadequacies of life with which we meet, to the detriment of individual and public welfare. Wherever we turn we meet with such incompetency and inefficiency in the work of every class of society, and this inefficiency springs mainly from a want of thoroughness, in the first instance, owing to the faulty development of the sense of Truth. Such inefficient men have no desire to know either their trade, their business or their profession or the relation which they hold to it; and such incompetence will be found in every class. Most of the losses we sustain, the annoyances we experience and the resentment with which criminal pretence fills us are due to this want of thoroughness and efficiency. The artisan and craftsman, who, after imperfect apprenticeship, boldly flounder into work of a subtle and valuable nature, unable to carry it to completion while destroying precious material; the foreman and contractor, and even the architect, who, ignorant of the constructive nature of the material with which they are dealing, undertake an order far beyond their capacity; the manufacturer and the merchant who remain content with the mere business manipulation, which alluringly tempts them into speculation promising rapid acquisition of wealth, without grasping, by searching and persevering study, the true nature of the goods themselves which they are supposed to produce or to manipulate; the shopkeeper and his clerk who know and care nothing about the wares they sell and whose function is merely idly to wait for a customer and then practise vulgar and inept arts of rhetoric and persuasion; the lawyer who is no jurist; the medical practitioner who is no true man of science and remains content with the empirical remedies which he has acquired in his apprenticeship, unacquainted with the true principles of his science and its progress, and therefore unable to cope with unforeseen conditions which the physiological and pathological processes of human life are bound to produce; the politician who is no statesman, and the soldier who takes no real interest in the art and science of war—these are the curses of modern society, because they live a lie and know not what is Truth. It is this want of thoroughness, this amateurishness, in the traditions of our life-work, which is our national weakness, as the tradition of thorough ness was the strength of the Germany of old[1], lowered and defiled in the changed mentality of the latter-day Germany, whose ideals of efficiency were established by the lowering of their conception of Truth,—though whatever successes they may have achieved in this war have been due to the inheritance of the spirit of thoroughness established by the older Germany, which the wave of modern *Strebertum* has not been able entirely to submerge.

Now this want of thoroughness in our traditions of work is in no way due to deficiency in the element of perseverance, tenacity and seriousness of purpose in our national character. On the contrary, we possess these qualities to the very highest degree, as is shown by our success in all efforts which require moral courage and tenacity, even in our industrial and commercial life as well as in our enterprise as a seafaring and colonising nation, and our *ultimate* success in the struggle with other nations both in peace and in war. It is due, not to the want of force, but to the want of direction in which this force is used, to the irrational traditions, to the unwillingness—in fact to the direct dislike—of the national genius to face and to grasp theory and all that is abstract. These national habits and traditions have produced what Meredith called "England's hatred of thought." We remain satisfied with the hand-to-mouth process of evolving our theory out of our practice, of raising "expediency" to the highest level of our intellectual aspirations, and of practising an opportunism, which may for the moment produce illusory and ephemeral success at the cost of lasting achievement and progress. Above all, this national failing is due to the fundamentally fallacious principles of our educational system with its mercenary and pandering appeal to the lower instincts

---

[1] Cf. *Aristodemocracy*, Chaps. II., III.

and the ignorant cupidity of the vulgar mass of the people. And it is these same erroneous and misguiding principles which are invoked at this moment, when, in the painful recognition of our inefficiency, there arises a loud clamour to reform our national education by learning a lesson from our German enemies. When we demand that our educational training should take direct cognisance of the needs of our individual life and should directly prepare the young for the satisfaction of these needs, we fail to see that we begin at the wrong end and must entirely reverse our order of thought. We wish to bring science and our intellectual life down to the needs of our commercial and industrial life. The methods of German national education, which underlie all the commercial and the industrial, as well as the military, successes of that nation, consisted in the systematic endeavour to raise the economic and the industrial life of the people upwards into direct and efficient touch with the highest and purest practices and achievements of science. To do this, the people as a whole and the national consciousness had to be made acquainted with, or at least, to be put into intellectual sympathy with, the highest and purest thought, and to learn to understand, to honour and to love it. Theory and research, as pursued by the chief votaries of Science, and practised in their universities, were brought in touch with the mass of the population. Instead of hatred of thought and of theory as a national—in fact as a social—characteristic of the people at large, there grew up respect for knowledge, the consciousness, moreover, that these remote spheres of mental activity and of intellectual achievement were friendly powers which could be appealed to, and could be used, even for the humblest form of daily activities in trade, industry and commerce. The result has been the facile, ready and all-pervading application of science to industry, and, above all, the spirit of thoroughness in the teaching of every subject, from the highest academic teaching, through the technical and secondary schools, to the elementary schools[1]. Still more important in its all-pervading, though not so apparent, results has been the realisation of the true nature, as well as the material value, of the highest ideals of scientific Truth. No knowledge is firmly founded and thoroughly acquired unless it can be reduced to first principles. Therefore no workman can undertake a definite task unless he has thoroughly mastered the elements of the material upon which he is working and the methods of the work itself. This forms the distinction between the amateur and the professional worker.

Importance of the Humanities. But we have said above that the business of life includes our dealing in business with our fellow-men. The goods which are produced or transported from the producer to the consumer, the markets which create the demand or may be opened up by the judicious efforts of the producer and the merchant, are made for human beings and for human society, as they are produced and transported by human beings. The needs of these human beings must therefore be considered in the production of such goods, and the nature of these human beings must be considered in the distribution. We do not go far wrong if we maintain that one half of the important industrial and commercial functions, both in the

[1] For a previous discussion of this question see my article on "The Ideal of a University" (*North American Review*, September, 1903): also *The Study of Art in Universities*, Harper & Bros, 1896, pp. 51–70; see also two Notes (C and D) from that book, as well as an article on "Educational Reform" from the *Journal of Education*, June, 1916, here reprinted in the Appendix.

production and the distribution of goods, is concerned with the just and adequate understanding of human nature and human life and our power of dealing with these. I am not merely considering that vast class in the production of human commodities, in which the element of human taste and preference is the chief motive to production, or affects to a greater or a lesser degree the objects which are produced, but I am considering merely the relation which the production of goods holds to the understanding of human nature and human life, and, especially, to the importance which the correct estimate of human nature has in the distribution of goods and in our business dealing with other human beings. Thus, even in our business life, in industry and in commerce, the knowledge of man is of supreme importance. This knowledge of man is directly furthered by all those studies which we call the Humanities, and the study of man, his thoughts and language, his private, social and political life in the past and present. It need hardly be insisted upon, that, in the preparation of the efficient worker in any and in every sphere of life, this element is of supreme importance; nor need I justify my contention that in the production of all those articles which are meant wholly or in part to satisfy human taste, the acquisition of taste, manifested in its purest and most potent form in the art and literature of the world is, if not absolutely essential, at all events, emphatically useful. But finally it must be conceded—and this will receive fuller treatment in the next chapter—that the power of formulating our ideas clearly and expressing them in logical and intelligible speech, is not only of considerable importance in our business dealings, but is also directly conducive to clearness of thought, as well as to the methods and the thorough apprehension of Truth. The educational value of the study of language as the chief vehicle in the expression of human thought is undeniable. We may go further and say, that in using language, the less we consider it merely as a means for the expression of our desires (the desires and not the expression being uppermost in our consciousness) the greater is the educational and disciplinary value of the study of language in forming the habits of mind which make for thoroughness, accuracy and the higher appreciation of Truth. Therefore the study of foreign languages and the accurate and searching effort to understand the thoughts of others and adequately to convey them, in another vehicle, is most important as a discipline, apart from the immediate uses and social advantages which the knowledge of foreign tongues may bring. On the same grounds, however, the study of so-called dead languages, unadulterated by the intrusion of desires and use, becomes especially important and effective. The perfect organisation of classical studies, developed through ages by the efforts of foremost scholars, furnishes us with an instrument of education which it is unlikely that we can replace by any substitute. Quite apart from the inestimable advantage to the spread and advancement of culture, intellectual refinement and taste which they bring, the mental effort of accurately rendering the meaning of a Greek or Latin author into intelligible English, and even of converting our thoughts into the remote, though ever-living, perfect and refined instrument of ancient Greek and Latin, is a training in precision and concentration of thought and its expression, tending towards the ultimate refinement of our sense of Truth, which it would be a decided loss for civilised humanity to forgo.

CHAPTER VII.

JUSTICE AND CHARITY

In the previous chapter we have been dealing with man's relation to Truth in the business of life and, further, with his attitude towards other human beings from this point of view, in order that his mental training should lead to efficiency. But there is another side to his relationship to his fellow-men, in addition to his business relation, in fact, in its spirit and nature exclusive of this "interested" attitude of mind—i.e. his social relationship to them. However important the serious business side of life may be, it is not an exaggeration to say that half man's efforts, half his conscious and subconscious desires, are purely concerned with his social relationship to his fellow-men, and that, ultimately, even as a result of his efforts in the business of life, these latter are measured by their bearings upon his social relation, upon the approval or esteem in which others hold him and on the position which he can command in the society of which he is a member. The truth of this statement is supported by Aristotle's definition of man as a "social animal," as his essential and distinctive attribute, differentiating him from the animal world. At all events, this aspect of his conscious activity may claim equal importance with that which leads to efficiency. As a matter of fact, much of even this efficiency will depend upon the perfect development of his social qualities. While the bulk of ethics, which are the guide to his moral conduct, is thus concerned with the social relation between men, with man in action, with the regulation of these acts so as to produce an ideal state of human society, and is thus eminently practical (so that Kant designated his ethical inquiries by the title *Critique of Practical Reason* in contradistinction to his *Critique of Pure Reason*), it is even here—perhaps above all here— that the correct conception, appreciation and application of Truth is of supreme effect and importance. For, without the faculties that make for and command Truth, our charitable impulses, our social instincts and training, may fail us, as they undoubtedly often do, in our dealings with our fellow- men, especially when our selfish passions, and above all the most active and destructive of our social vices, jealousy and envy, dominate us.

Justice a Matter of Understand- ing. Our judgment of other people, and the re- lation which we ought to hold to them and they to us, are entirely warped by these passions. It is only by the help of our reason, of our intellectual grasp of Truth, that these errors and crimes can be rectified, as it is only by the formation of the habit of mind which enables us at all times to appeal to, and to apply, our apprehension of Truth, that justice in our dealing with our fellow-men is ensured and that true and effective charity can be exercised. Such justice is ultimately not a matter of feeling, but of understanding.

Social Pre- judice and Convention. To begin with the proper estimate of other people, it requires, above all things, the elimination of prejudice. The wildest and most common form of social prejudice is in the ignorant or thoughtless acceptance of adventitious attributes, assigning social qualities or faults, virtues or vices, privileges or penalties, which may have had some remote justification for groups of individuals under conditions of life long since past, but which in no way apply to the individuals of whose moral or social qualities we are now to judge. This leads to that form of social prejudice which has been stigmatised as "snobbishness." We begin with the establishment of false values and we proceed to the misapplication of even these values to those with whom we have to deal. Even when the general marks of value on the broadest, rough and ready and inaccurate fixing of them by outer material conditions or by the hasty judgment of public bodies, have set their guinea-stamp upon the gold, and in so far (when opportunities are not afforded to recognise it as gold or to test its true value) may be accepted and may be of use—there is no need for this guinea-stamp when opportunity and even duty force us to test the true gold value. But in the ordinary thoughtless course of life, with those whose sense of Truth has not been developed and is not effectively present in their *moral*, the adventitious guinea-stamp overrules their acknowledgment of the inferior metal, which it untruthfully raises in value, while the pure gold which they have tested carries no value to them when it is not marked by the vulgar misleading stamp. The whole balance of justice in the social estimates of ordinary life is thus upset, and prejudice and injustice divert the flow of social existence into tortuous channels, polluting the clearness of its stream.

Self-detach-ment and Justice leading to Charity.
If such are the vices and deficiencies of our social attitude when not directed by Truth in their general form and widest grouping, injustice and unkindness in our particular dealings with individuals are still more frequently the result of thoughtlessness and the absence of truthfulness in our judgment of our fellow-men. Intellectual altruism, the exercise of

our altruistic imagination, is the safest guide to social justice. The "golden rule" has long since impressed the truth of this fact. To see in their true light the claims of others and our own in due proportion to one another, is the essence of all justice in our dealings. But the effectiveness and realisation of justice depend upon our understanding, upon our training in apprehending Truth and upon our adherence to its highest and purest standards. To attain to these, as we have seen, depends upon the elimination of our own prejudices and desires which block the way to perfect understanding. More positively it implies the power of self-detachment, of stepping outside ourselves, which our theoretical and imaginative faculties enable us to do. As this mental habit helps us to check our selfish impulses which lead us to harm others, so it also induces us to forgive the harm that may be done to us. *Tout comprendre c'est tout pardonner* remains one of the truest of commonplaces. Thus, through this same faculty of self-detachment, Justice meets, and is merged in, Charity, and confirms and strengthens the impulse of love which is as elementary and powerful in man as is that of hate and envy.

Love and hate are the two ruling passions in man and may be of equal strength. No doubt, however, some are born with a preponderance of hate in their natures, while some are originally of a more loving disposition, others, again, are strong and passionate in their feelings or feeble and cold in temperament. There are no doubt those who are endowed from birth with affectionate dispositions, loving natures. Kindness and generosity may thus dwell in the breast of an illiterate clown to a greater degree and more effectively than in that of a cultured peer. But there comes a phase in the more complex conduct of social life when thoughtfulness and

the power of apprehending Truth are essential to justice and
even to charity in action, and when without them our native
disposition is not enough to guide us: the ignorant and untrained are then helplessly carried away by instinct and
passion. The strength of love over hate is Truth which produces justice and charity. Therefore in the struggle between
love and hate love must prevail in the end. To put it into
a quasi-mathematical equation: If love originally equals
hate as a passion, love has in addition reason, thought and
truth, which produce justice, to strengthen it and give it
endurance and lasting power. Love + Truth = Justice and
Charity; Hate − Truth = Injustice and Envy. Love endures; but it must be founded on Truth. Without the power
of apprehending Truth, neither Justice nor Love endures.

Thus in our dealings with our fellow-men the
*Calumny and
Slander.* development of our sense of truth is most
effective, though perhaps in a more indirect
and remote process of application. We come, however, much
nearer to its more direct effect when our judgments of our
fellow-men are expressed by us in words and are communicated to others whose estimate is thus directly influenced
by such transmitted judgment. As has been pointed out in
the opening chapters, it is here that often the lowest standards of morality obtain among those who in all other respects manifest higher morality in their convictions and in
their conduct. This is, I maintain, due to the fact that their
estimate of truth is not adequate, and that the search for
truth and its application to life have not, by a refined and
continuous training, been made habitual in their mentality
as a whole. It leads, as I have indicated in the Introduction,
to degradation and to misery, to the disturbance and the
lowering of the peaceful flow of social life, and is more widespread and intense than is realised by the greater number of

people. It covers all that may be summarised under the term slander. Now, we may at once exclude wilful calumny, the attempt, with deliberate forethought, to harm another by misrepresentation of facts. But outside the mephitic domain of actual calumny there is a vast region of untruthful statements to the detriment of our fellow-men with dangerous hillocks and vague and doubtful plains and morasses of untruth, which people traverse heedlessly, not realising the traces which their footprints leave and the evil effects upon their own health which such a journey entails. The motives to such evil action vary from more or less conscious jealousy and hatred to thoughtlessness, from the craving for witty and humorous conversation and the amusement it gives, to mere talkativeness; but the harm which is done remains and is often out of all proportion to the lightness of the impulse which gave it birth.

In its worst form, approaching more or less closely to direct calumny, the first impulse to slander—or to use the more appropriate French word *"médisance"*—is given by jealousy or envy. But it differs from calumny in that the evil motive is not fully conscious as the untruthfulness is not deliberately present to the mind. But from the most violent forms of these evil passions, there is a gradual shading off to their almost imperceptible and unconscious presence in the lighter form—not devoid of some mitigating humour —which prevents us from denying to ourselves some slight pleasure in the discomfiture of our best friends—provided always they are successful in life. So active and widespread is this motive in human nature, that I have occasionally tried the experiment of predicting how long it would take,— in the case of very prominent and successful men and women who were made the idols of an appreciative and grateful public while they were achieving, or just after they had achieved, success,—to discover a reactionary wave of criticism and detraction, culminating often in grave charges and in most ludicrous untruths. I should not like to illustrate *in corpore vili* the vice of over-generalisation, to which I have referred above, by an overstatement which I make myself. But I am tempted to say that in almost every case my prediction proved true. To point it with two striking examples: Immediately following on their public successes in certain stages of their careers I discovered a wave of unfriendly criticism in various layers of society directed against both Lord Roberts and Lord Kitchener. No doubt the effect of such *médisance* was limited in extent and temporary; but the interesting and significant feature of the phenomenon was that it followed immediately upon their successful achievements and universal commendation.

In the lighter forms, however, of mere tittle-tattle, thoughtlessly originated and thoughtlessly repeated and diffused, slander is so common in every layer of society that its effects are not only most disturbing to the peace and prosperity of social life, but act in a degrading and coarsening manner upon the social tone in lowering the prevailing standards of Truth, and demoralising and disintegrating to the sense of veracity in the slanderers themselves. This sin is in the first instance due to the want of altruistic imagination. If the originators or *colporteurs* of slander were for a moment to apply the Golden Rule, and attempt to realise how it would feel if such things were to be said about themselves, if their own trustworthiness and honour as men and women were assailed, if the result were to ruin or impair their social position, the serious business of life, if it entailed the loss of personal friends and acquaintances,—it might fairly be doubted whether most of the people who lightly make or repeat damaging statements would do so. Yet if we

look about us, we find that in every social centre in the
country, from the smallest village to the great metropolis,
from the circles in which move the highest of the land down
to the life "below stairs," the constant and frivolous assertions of untruths or, at least, of gross inaccuracies, are
lightly made and are received with greedy readiness, and
that they frequently result in untold misery and in the unhappiness of innocent people and often in the destruction of
their usefulness in life. Though most of us will at once
realise that it is wrong to invent lies about our neighbours and
to communicate them to others, there are few who consider
their grave responsibilities in repeating and in spreading
them[1], and still fewer again who are alive to the fact that
it is their duty (however much they may shrink from disturbing the grace of social intercourse by tactless and
awkward denials) to dispel or to modify a statement which
they have reason to know is untrue, or even to challenge a
damaging statement of which a doubt may exist in their
minds. But the fact remains that it is perfectly possible,
without sinning against good manners or impairing the
general social tone for which we are all responsible, thus to
protest, to correct or to express our doubt.

There is here a vast sphere of "sins of omission," sins in
which we become "accessories to the crime." We will sit by
with folded hands and hear the most damaging statements
made about people and even about our tested friends, feel
the injustice, or, at least, have our doubts as to whether an
injustice is not being committed, and not lift a finger to

---

[1] Cicero (*De Rep.* IV. 10) refers to the punishment of the author of
a *carmen famosum*, including even him who distributed it. The
actio famosa included those who helped the author. In the Theodosian
Code and by an edict of Valentinian and Valens capital punishment
was even meted out to him, who having found a libel, communicated
it instead of destroying it.

protect those who, where truth is concerned, are always in
need of such protection. The phrase "Mind your own business," or "it's none of my business" is accountable for much
that is vile and cowardly. It is as wrong to sit silent and, by
one's silence, to confirm the spread of an untruth, as it is
selfish and morally irresponsible to meet the undoubted
proofs of the unworthiness and indignity of a dishonourable
man unfit for decent society, by a shrug of the shoulder and
the words "he has always been quite pleasant to me."
There are many Dreyfus cases constantly developing in our
midst the tragic issues of which on a smaller scale would
never have come to fruition if we who knew the truth or
could help it to prevail did not give tacit assent by our
inaction; as the social success of many a dishonourable
impostor, or even criminal, would never be possible if we
did not put the seal of our approval upon him by suppressing
our protest or even by admitting him into our society. Were
our children to be taught at school and at home, and were
such teaching to be continued by scrupulous practice in
after life, that it is as dishonest and dishonourable to make
damaging statements about our neighbours, as it is to deceive and to cheat or to steal; and were this to be instilled by
every means into the daily life of all classes, much harm and
misery would be avoided—while the sense of Truth within
the nation would be kept purer, higher and more effective.

It is, after all, here that the evil lies; in the lowness of our
conception, and the bluntness of our sense, of Truth. Most
people are not taught and trained to realise that they have no
right to make any statement as a fact which they have not
tested as being true. This, again, depends upon our intellectual
standards in relation to words and language, as much as
active morality depends upon our moral standard in our deeds.

CHAPTER VIII.

TRUSTWORTHINESS[1]

The Truthful and the Untruthful. THE effectiveness of our conception and practice of Truthfulness in social life, as regards our attitude towards others, depends, after all,

[1] I am not here dealing with questions of moral casuistry concerning Truth—cases in which we are justified in telling an untruth. I may as well quote a passage from *Aristodemocracy* (pp. 258–9; see also *Patriotism, National and International*, the chapter on "The Ascending Scale of Corporate Duties," pp. 101 seq.): "The way to deal with such moral casuistics is the purely positive, and not the negative method. By that I mean that one valid moral injunction is not eliminated by the fact of its clashing with another. Each one remains valid; though at times reason and the application of a general sense of justice and proportion may have to decide whether the one injunction is not stronger than the other. 'Thou shalt not lie' retains its validity, even though 'Thou shalt not endanger the life and the permanent happiness of another' may lead the physician or the friend for the nonce to tell an untruth to an insane person or an invalid when the truth would undermine life or life's efficiency. A practical moral test can always be transmitted to the pupil, in bringing him conscientiously to ask himself whether, imagining that when the cause which led him to tell such an untruth or to commit an infraction of an ethical law is removed, he would be prepared to lay before the person to whom he told the untruth or to independent and disinterested people whom he respects, the course of action which he had pursued."

By means of the just application of the principles of "The Ascending Scale of Duties" all the problems implied in cases in which we are justified, and even bound, to tell an untruth are thus solved without impairing the validity of our duty to tell the truth. The cases in which an unjustified question is put, when we have clearly manifested our intention and our right to withhold information, the guarding of the author's pseudonym in the case of the Waverley Novels and similar well-known instances, as well as conventional phrases, such as "Dear Sir," "Yours sincerely," "Not at home," etc., in no way affect the validity of the moral law which enjoins the duty to speak the truth.

upon the degree in which Truth rules within us, and our character shows itself to the outer world in our adherence to its dictates. The man of honour, the wholly trustworthy person, is he whose "word is as good as his bond." The man who never knowingly tells an untruth, who even does not profess to know what he does not know and does not overstate what he does know, is trustworthy, is the man of strictest honesty. The honest man is he who, in words as well as in deeds, is clearly himself and does not wish to appear to be what he is not, to possess what he does not own, and to know what he does not know—this is the truly trustworthy man.

Yet how few are there who, though they may never deliberately or consciously tell a falsehood, are accurate in their statements of facts, careful to qualify these statements so as never to mislead by exaggeration, and ever ready to admit their ignorance? The difference between men of such high standards and their less perfect fellow-men is not only that existing between the literate and illiterate, the educated and untrained minds, the thoughtful and the thoughtless, but between the truthful and the untruthful.

Exaggeration of Truthful Conscientious-ness. Now we must at once guard against over-stating our case as we must admit that, if these moral injunctions with regard to truth were to lead to constant or inopportune self-searching and to excess of caution and hesitancy, resulting from the desire to weigh each statement in the balance of accurate thought, it would deprive us of all spontaneity in expression and in conversation, and make of us either tiresome pedants or inarticulate stammerers in thought and in speech, while it would banish from conversation all wit and humour and even all grace, and thus impoverish or weigh down the free growth and flowering of social life. We may thus err on the other side and become cumbrous pedants or even self-deceiving Pharisees, who humbly, though assertively, qualify all their statements about the outer world and about themselves, generally obtruding their own personality where its presence is in no way called for. "Unworthy as I am" (when he is not, or certainly ought not to be), "though I know nothing about this subject" (when he does know, or ought to know), "you all know more than I do" (which he certainly does not believe, or if he does believe it, it ought to reduce him to silence)—all such phrases are not only unnecessary, but are generally in themselves insincere, and certainly do not add to the spontaneous and graceful flow of human intercourse, nor even do they favour fulness in conversation. The constant qualification of every ordinary statement, the cowardly avoidance of taking the responsibility for a definite pronouncement, the checking or flattening of all uprisings into the playful ripplings or graceful soarings of the flow and flights of wit and humour, would indeed reduce all statement to a fluid or gelatinous condition eluding all endeavours to hold and to retain what is stated. Social intercourse would certainly become either unbearable or be robbed of all its vitality and grace.

The same applies to literature, to the written word and to style. If the effort to conform to the higher dictates of veracity leads to platitudinarianism; to the iteration of truisms; to the weighing down of every statement by involved qualifications, parentheses and discursive limitations; to the overloading of sentences with redundant adjectives and qualifying adverbs (of which, I fear, I am myself here and elsewhere giving abundant illustration)—the style and the substance conveyed by it will lose their power and purpose, and we long even for the faults of coarse exaggeration, for overstatement and paradox which are the besetting sins of modern literature.

The Assertive Dogmatist. Nevertheless, the assertive and dogmatising man, the thumping, domineering over-stater, the omniscient person, the man who never admits his ignorance, are not only glaringly untrustworthy in diction and in character, but are ungainly and intellectually repulsive, as they spoil and even make quite impossible agreeable social intercourse[1]. This also applies to a whole group of intellectuals whose conversation is chiefly directed by their endeavour to escape from any subject of which they do not feel themselves complete masters, and to push or drag or inveigle it into spheres and on matters where they can do all the crowing and where they feel themselves the "cocks of the walk." More innocent, though equally tedious if not repulsive, is the dealer in superlatives; the man who knows everybody worth knowing and knows them intimately; whose friends are the greatest and best and most distinguished; whose every possession or purchase is the best; and who emphasises his every statement with the most impressive adjuncts of asseveration or assurance. Whatever other qualities such people have they certainly do not include a refined sense of truthfulness, and they cannot command faith in their statements, however much we may trust their kindness of heart and their general good-nature. What, however, is more serious is their unconsciousness of the fact that, by deviating from the truth, they are habitually committing a crime; and that, by our admission or toleration of such delinquencies and weaknesses we are lowering our

[1] See Appendix IV (article on "Modesty" in *Harper's Weekly*).

general standards of Truth, the maintenance of which on a
supreme level is of the utmost importance.

So also in literature, the dominance of the
Exaggeration and Paradox in Literature. paradox, the mentality from which it emanates
as well as the mental *ethos* which it tends to
produce in the public, constitute a grave
menace to taste as well as to morality. Its origin is not due
to any intrinsic, artistic or literary principle or force; but
chiefly to the accident of the surface conditions of modern
material life. Exaggeration to arrest attention, and even
exaggeration as a legitimate element in humour, are the
strong drink of unsensitive palates, the flaring colours and
designs for eyes deadened in their visual perception by the
vulgar glare of modern life and the coarseness of touch of the
man whose whole life leads him to grope through the bustle
of crowded streets and mass-meetings. Literature, as monopolised by the newspaper and its style[1], becomes that of the
advertising agent, whose signboards have as their sole object
the arresting of attention. The result is, both in literature and
in art, the era of striking and sight-arresting lines, contrasted
masses unrelated and unharmonised, glaring colours, devoid
of tone, with unadjusted values, and the absence of refinement and harmony in design and in line, in shadings and in
half tones—in short want of refinement and accuracy. To
a great extent, though perhaps not wholly so, this disease
in taste, this practice of overstatement, this concentrated
and inordinate desire to arrest attention,—all these are due
to the fundamental habit of mind in which the sense of
Truth is not developed, but has been even coarsened.

If our habits of thought and expression, our whole mentality, were to be transfused with the highest conception of

[1] See Part II, below.

Truth which each age clearly formulates and brings within effective range of its thought and life in every phase of its activity, even the most remote from theory, the most practical, our tone of conversation and our taste in literature and art would be more adequately expressive of the truly best that is in us.

Conversation[1]. To complete this outline exposition of our subject a few remarks must be added on the relation of conversation to Truth. Conversation has been

---

[1] One of my learned friends, at the same time a brilliant conversationalist, has laid it down that the first rule of conversation was not to be accurate. Like most *mots* of that kind, this one contains a grain of truth. The belief of many tediously prosy and pedantic conversationalists that they must convey in one long-winded breath and soliloquy the final truth on every subject they touch upon, implies a finality in their own diction which leads to dogmatism as it springs from pedantry and egotism. But the brilliant and ready epigrammatist and lover of the inaccurate is equally dogmatic and also puts an end to all conversation of a serious and entertaining nature. To recall instances from those who are no more, the late Henry Sidgwick was as witty a man, possessed of as catholic a sense of humour as were few people whom I have known. But he was always fair and sympathetic to his interlocutor or adversary in a discussion, never overstating his case and always bringing the conversation as a whole nearer the goal of Truth. This did not exclude the epigram, wit or satire with their exaggeration and inaccuracy. These are fully justified from a literary and artistic point of view and can never be spared. They are to be considered, as it were, n quotation marks, or as in literature and art the caricature, the satire, the fantastic and grotesque are justified. The conversation of the late Oscar Wilde and that of his followers and imitators abounded in epigrams, until these became the very heart and substance of conversation instead of its pleasing and diverting adjuncts. They are the *hors d'œuvres* and *entremets* to the conversational meal. But a whole dinner consisting of nothing but such *hors d'œuvres* and *entremets* is not only not sustaining (as it is bad for the digestion), but becomes tediously irritating and not at all delectable to the palate—in fact a nauseating surfeit from which the hungry guests turn with the loss of all appetite.

defined by Plato and Aristotle as the means of arriving at the truth by the co-operation of two or more people, who enumerate facts and interchange views and opinions for this final purpose. It aims at the evolution of Truth by such discussion (Arist. *fr.* 54). Plato thus assigns the highest place among all sciences to conversation (διαλεκτική) and considers it the coping-stone (θριγκός) to all studies (*Rep.* 534 E). The chief object to be held in view, to which all others must be subordinated, is the discovery and the confirmation of Truth; and though, to arrive at it, each participant must express with adequate clearness his own experiences and opinions to carry understanding and conviction and also to point out error in the statement or argument of the other participants, in so far as it is not a monologue, but a dialogue, this is not the final aim: the real object is discovery of Truth, to which the conversation as a whole must be scrupulously subordinated. In every phase of conversation the participant ought to be conscious of this final purpose and ought never to act like a special-pleading lawyer or a casuistic disputant, who cares naught for Truth, but is bent merely upon asserting and carrying his own point. Our ultimate aim must be to add our share to the final discovery of Truth—to converse, not to cavil (οὐκ ἐρίζειν ἀλλὰ διαλέγεσθαι, Plato, *Rep.* 454 A).

Yet how rare is it to find this conscious or subconscious aim dominating a conversation! The desire to arrive at the truth is entirely lost sight of in the hurried eagerness of self-assertion and the consequent attempt to establish and to win recognition for hasty statements. Coupled with this, mark the eager, often meanly puerile, attempts at tripping up the adversary, the wilful misunderstanding, or even the perversion of his meaning; the merciless falling upon his

weak points, the unfair use that is made of a slip on his part
or an awkwardness in his turn of expression, lending itself
to cheap witticism, diverting the trend of thoughts from the
main issue and disconcerting the blunderer in exposition,
who may be sincerely bent upon arriving at the truth! How
one loves the man who, in a discussion, turns to his adversary
and remarks: "By the way, a very strong point in favour of
your contention is," etc.; who admits the strength of what
his opponent upholds, before expressing his doubts of its
validity—in short, the generous rival! I shall always hold
in pious memory the days of my early youth, when (more
than forty years ago) in the distinguished circle of intellectual
luminaries at George Henry Lewes' house "The Priory" in
London, George Eliot gave the most vital illustration of the
qualities of the true conversationalist in support of my own
weakness. I had come to England as a very young man from
a continuous stay of over three years at several German
universities, speaking and reading nothing but German and
dwelling exclusively in an atmosphere of German thought,
and had seriously impaired the spontaneity of expression in
my native tongue. I shall never forget, how, when in this
disconcerting position among my elders and intellectual
superiors, I ventured haltingly and blunderingly to express
my own opinions, she would then come to my rescue, and,
with delicate tact, suffused with kindliness and with pene-
trative intellectual sympathy, and with her mellow voice and
mellifluous though precise diction, would give perfect, lucid
form to my own involved thoughts—leaving me with increased self-confidence, almost proud of the pertinence and
importance of my own remarks. How grateful I was to her,
how I loved her—and how much she contributed, by her

unselfish intellectualism and passion for Truth, to the flow
and elevation of the conversation itself!

How rare it is to find a good listener! I mean by this, one
who dispels from his mind for a moment the urgent and
absorbing appeal of his own thoughts and his impulses of
self-expression, in order truly and fully to understand the
meaning and the drift of thought of his interlocutor. Before
the speaker has fairly begun most people are already entirely occupied with what they intend to answer. Watch
their faces, examine their eyes, and you will meet with no
sign of attention, no effort to grasp what is being said to
them. Most people we meet have preoccupied eyes. It is
above all in children that we meet with that pure, direct
look which goes out from them to the person or the thing
they are endeavouring to understand, entirely absorbed in
the object which their senses and their growing intellect are
trying to grasp in its true essence. One does meet this fresh-
ness and directness of the look in the eye of some admirable
people with pure or loving, or great and strong souls; but
above all, in wise men, however old they may be, who have
retained the heart and the enthusiasm of the child. But we
can all produce in ourselves this cardinal virtue, as it mani-
fests itself in the highest of human organs, by, on the one
hand, persistently checking and driving back the impulses to
self-absorption and, on the other hand, by an effort of will
(which, if continuously exercised, may ultimately produce
habit), by forcing our attention wholly to follow and to
grasp what is being communicated to us by others—above all,
by cultivating and strengthening our passion for Truth.

Reading.   As in conversation, so there is an application
of the same principle and motive-power to our
reading, of which modern men and women have made com-

paratively so great a practice; for the average adult, and
even youth, of every class in our days reads infinitely more
than did his forefathers. Most of these assiduous readers,
especially women, read for mere diversion; and this diversion
consists in satisfying, without effort, their hunger for the
coarser forms of wonder, of the unexpected, of what is purely
imaginative, sensational or humorous, or (when they venture
into the domain of thought) to find—again without effort—
their own thoughts reflected or confirmed by others. How
few of them are urged on to read continuously and with concentration in order that they may *learn*: that they may
increase the very narrow horizon of their experiences and
thoughts, that they may sharpen and refine their instruments of reason and their appreciation of Truth. Their
horror of what they call obscurity in a writer is in no way
limited to the justified instances where the author himself
has, from incompetence or from indolence, failed to give
clearness to the expression of his own thoughts; but emphatically extends to all writings where the subject-matter
itself, in its depths or in its elevation, requires, not only in
the adequate expression of it, but in the understanding of
its meaning and purport, an effort of concentration and
penetration which excludes all preoccupation, as it demands
serious and disciplined mental exertion. Men, on the other
hand, who from their school-days upwards have had the
advantage of higher education, have learnt the practice of
concentrated reading for their definite studies. Happily,
within the last generation or two, women are being trained
on the same lines; but the habit and the faculty are rarely
kept up and improved in after life. Would it not be possible
for women with any intellectual aspirations or claims to
culture, who are possessed of leisure, to devote one hour, or

even half-an-hour, a day habitually to read some serious book with the same concentration, in the same spirit, as marked their earlier studies? The boy and the man who have known the delight of fretting and puzzling over an obscure passage in Greek or in some modern philosophical author, resulting in the final victory in which they have been able to render the true meaning in their own language, and fulfilled the serious task which their life-work in those days imposed upon them, will have given birth in their own soul to a passion, which among all human passions is least likely to injure their neighbours or to degrade their own loftiness of soul—the passion for Truth.

But what is the meaning of all these various manifestations in our inner life, in our business and in our social life, which lead to honesty, to efficiency, to justice and charity, to trust-worthiness and honour and to our faculty of furthering the amenities of social intercourse? They are all focussed on the one great achievement of the human mind, our ruling passion for Truth, underlying and guiding all work, all intercourse, all conversation, the highest form of moral and intellectual unselfishness and of beneficent altruism.

PART II.

PUBLIC VERACITY

CHAPTER I.

GENERAL IMPORTANCE OF PUBLIC VERACITY

WHAT has been said of Truth in the life of the individual applies also—perhaps even more potently—to public veracity. Truth is the greatest material asset of individual and public life. Trust and confidence are the foundation of all fair business dealing as they are of social intercourse. Like the protection of life and property they must be guarded by law and custom. Children must be taught, and adults must be confirmed in their conviction, that lying is as pernicious and far-reaching a crime as theft and murder. The State must directly and positively guard Truth as much as life and property.

Morality thus applies to public as much as it does to private life. In the classical pronouncement of President Wilson he maintains "that we are at the beginning of an age in which it will be insisted that the same standards of conduct and responsibility for wrong done shall be observed among nations and their governments that are observed among individual citizens of civilised States."

We may go further and say that it ought to be and is in the very nature of things more possible for the laws of morality to prevail within the larger corporate bodies and among States than among individuals. The larger public bodies and States are not more, but less, likely to be tempted

to sin against Truth and Justice; and their morality ought
to be higher not lower than individual morality. For, in the
first place, corporate bodies are *directly* governed by laws,
whereas individuals, though *ultimately* subject to and controlled by such laws, legally and morally, are directly moved
to action by impulse, instinct and desire. interest or will. In
the second place, the conditions of corporate action, especially in modern democratic States, are such as to preclude the
influence of momentary caprice, the accidents of individual
temperament and the complexities of individual life. Furthermore, those who carry out and are responsible for the
corporate action of the State are forced to realise that every
act reflects upon public morality and public honour. If the
individual has to maintain his own and even his family
honour, the State is responsible for the national honour and
includes that of all its citizens. Finally a simple truth must
be recognised that, just as the religious life of the Church
should be higher and purer than that of its single votaries,
so must the morality of the State be higher than that of its
individual citizens.

Now it is essential to the normal life of a civilised and
democratic community that the citizen should have full
faith and confidence in the justice and veracity of the State.
The citizen of a democratic country should, by the constitution of the State, by its traditions and government and
by every individual public action, be confirmed in his conviction of the fairness, trustworthiness and truthfulness of
his political rulers. There can hardly be a greater shock to
the moral sense of modern man living in a modern democratic State than a case of miscarriage of justice. Though we
know that such an event is possible, in fact, that such
isolated accidents and exceptions in the administration of

the law governing civilised communities have occurred and do occur, our faith in the constraining rule, in its necessary logical sequence, in the rational causality, leads us to believe firmly in the supreme rule of justice; in fact, that though exceptional errors may occur, right will prevail in the end.

Without this fundamental belief our conscious existence would not be what it is. Of equal basic importance to the very nature of our civilised consciousness is our faith in the truthfulness of the State, that the State as such cannot lie. The individual may be unjust, the State can never be. There may be corrupt officials; but the State itself with its sovereignty must remain pure and truthful in our conception.

In the autocratic governments of the past a marked dualism, and even antagonism, between the governors and the governed was justified in fact, as it was encouraged by the attitude of such governments towards their subjects. Authority, power, force were the ground upon which obedience was exacted, and therefore the mental attitude of the subjects was either that of unreasoning obedience or of divergence and antagonism of interests, of resentment and revolt—the attitude of the slave to his master. In a democracy, government is established by consent, the governed delegate authority to the government, as they make their own laws. The government is a friend not an enemy of the people. It is therefore essential that the citizens should have faith in the justice, the absolute fairness and trustworthiness of the administrators of the law. Every act of the administration which destroys or weakens this faith dissolves the essence and spirit of democratic government. That a government should lie, should be unfair or tricky in its dealings, is a blow at the most vital organ of the body politic.

The government and the law-abiding citizens are thus co-operators in the furtherance of the objects of the State. It is only with the criminal and the law-breaker that the government is in conflict and is justified in using methods of warfare.

If these truths are so fundamental and self-evident that they inevitably sound like platitudes, the practice, if not the theory as well, of modern politics even in the most democratic States, does not always confirm and support such principles and beliefs.

CHAPTER II.

TRUTH IN INTERNATIONAL RELATIONSHIPS

To begin with the international relationships of States to one another, our public morality, more especially as regards veracity, is in direct contradiction with the ethical consciousness of modern man and the spirit of modern democracies. The traditions as well as the organisation of the Foreign Offices and the Diplomatic Services in the modern world, even in the most democratic States, with the Secret Service, the Military and other Attachés (whose function is in many cases that of spies even in times of peace), are entirely at variance not only with our convictions, but with our professions. Even in modern democratic States, in many aspects of our activities, we still stand on the ground of Machiavelli's *Principe*. It was a diplomat who said that: "*La parole a été donnée à l'homme pour cacher sa pensée.*" (Speech has been given to man to hide his thoughts.) We have all—though perhaps in different degrees—sinned in this respect. It is not merely for the immediate consequences in European history that the falsification of the Ems telegram by Bismarck and his colleagues marks a tragic downward step in the evolution of modern politics; but for its effect upon the political consciousness of modern man. When it stands in all its nakedness and degrading cynicism before our moral judgment, every normal moral being must be stirred to the depths and urged to moral revolt against the promulgation of an untruth.

If we could become acquainted with the true facts in the organisation of the German Secret Service as directed by von Holstein in the days of Bismarck (the details of which even the great statesman could not control) casting its net for many years all over the world in times of peace, the fearful duplicity and demoralisation of which are more and more coming to light in these latter days, the moral sense of every right-thinking man and woman in every country would be revolted. Shall we ever know the whole truth concerning the German preparation for this war and its inception, the direct activity, not so much of the *All-deutsche* party as of the Kaiser himself, of Prince Bülow, his colleagues and successors and the various Departments of State? Will the archives of the Foreign Office at Vienna and Berlin ever reveal all the secret documents which passed between them immediately before the war? We shudder at the cesspools of lying, at the duplicity and corruption which the Bolo affair and similar scandals that have come to light, reveal. Shall we ever know all about the atrocities in Belgium and in Northern France, and who was directly responsible for these dastardly crimes? At a recent Socialistic gathering at Berne a German Socialist Deputy categorically denied the truths of fact with regard to these atrocities and was evidently led to believe by the official communications in his own country that they had never occurred.

Even after the war, humanity must not forget the existence of such charges and must dispassionately establish the truth in order to right the balance of the world's morality. Professor Nippold has asserted in "*Das Erwachen des Deutschen Volkes und die Rolle der Schweiz*" (Zurich, 1917), that, had the truth been told to the German people, they would have awakened from the hypnotic sleep into which the official lies had put them and the war would never have taken place or, had it been begun, would have ended as soon as the truth was known.

Surely the free citizens of every country have not only the right, but the duty, to know and to discover the truth and to control the action of the State in what is most vital to their lives and their interests.

When in medicine a disease has actually manifested itself in an acute form, it generally calls for what might be termed a "symptomatic" treatment; there is no time for an organic or constitutional treatment. The world is now suffering from the severest of all the acute diseases, and the cure must in so far be symptomatic, i.e. decisive victory over the militaristic and autocratic enemy. But when this acute crisis in the health of civilised humanity has yielded to this heroic treatment, the time will come when we must investigate the more fundamental "etiology," the organic causes which led to the disease. Such an organic cause is the suppression of truth and the diffusion of falsehood.

When in the future—as we may all hope—a League of Nations, or, as I should prefer, an International Court backed by Power[1], is established, it will be one of the chief functions of such an international body to suppress untruths and to ensure the widest publication of truth. The difficult task will, of course, be, when the truth is determined, to ensure that it shall effectually be published and transmitted even into the culpable country and among its people against the will of the government without destroying or contravening the sovereignty of the State. But there is a very

---

[1] See my own plan for such an International Court as first given in *The Expansion of Western Ideals and the World's Peace*, 1899, pp. 105 seq.; and *Aristodemocracy*, etc., Chap. XI.

simple answer and expedient for such a doubt. For one of the inalienable rights of such an International Court will be that its decisions and findings and all the reports of its international work shall be published regularly and distributed throughout every country belonging to the League, and even in the countries that have not given their adherence. Such publication will be a regular part of its official functions. It will thus be far from one of the least important and effective functions of this body of the future to counteract the lie and to diffuse and confirm the reign of truth.

It is one of the many and most grave misfortunes of these latter days that the fight for universal rights admitted by all just and sane people is taken up by one section or one party in the several countries who may be in most other respects at variance with the rest of their fellow-citizens, and arouses artificial and irrational opposition where otherwise no such opposition could exist. The control of foreign affairs should never be made a party question; it is a fundamental right and duty of every citizen in a democratic country. We have done with the traditions of a lying diplomacy.

CHAPTER III.

TRUTH IN DOMESTIC POLITICS

THE importance of Truth in international relations will be readily admitted. In domestic politics its effect and influence manifest themselves not so directly in the promulgation or enforcement of definite national claims or interests and their transmission and publication, but in a more indirect and general, though none the less effective, way in the moral atmosphere produced by practice and tradition in the several departments of national administration.

We have insisted above on the importance of faith and confidence of the governed in their government, and have maintained that any actions, traditions or customs in governments which weaken or destroy this faith, are injurious to the essence of domestic government and demoralising to the national life of the people.

While considering the duties of man to the State[1], we must equally insist upon the moral duties of the State to its citizens. One of the primary duties of the State in this respect is that none of its institutions, traditions or actions should directly contravene the sense of justice, fairness and veracity. It need not be insisted upon that this applies above all to the administration of justice. But of less direct, though of equal importance, the several business departments in the administration of government must scrupulously and manifestly stand before the public in not only avoiding

---

[1] See *Aristodemocracy*, etc., Part IV. Chap. III.

all practices which would not be considered just and fair in the private dealings of honourable people; but they must positively and directly display the desire for fair, friendly and generous treatment of the citizens with whom they deal. Any procedure or custom or tradition in the working of such a department which implies unfair dealing, or is even remotely based on the assumption of an antagonistic or inimical attitude of the government towards the governed, is destructive of such faith and strikes the keynote of deception and untruthfulness in their dealings.

Now, rightly or wrongly, for instance, the opinion is widespread that the Treasury and the Inland Revenue Offices work upon the assumption that they must get the highest possible contribution out of the taxpayer, and that the taxpayer will avail himself of every chance to avoid the obligations which the law of the country places upon him. Apart from their legitimate duty to foil the attempts (which are moreover criminal) of the citizen who, by the suppression of truth or by actual deception, endeavours to evade the payment of his obligatory taxes, they are keenly and persistently bent upon detecting and pointing out any mistake he may have made to the detriment of the fiscus. On the other hand, no tradition seems to exist (or if it does the public is not made aware of it) voluntarily to detect and to make known any mistake that has been made to the illegitimate advantage of the Treasury and to the detriment of the taxed citizen. Moreover the procedure in rectifying such a mistake is so cumbersome and onerous that the citizen is often discouraged from attempting to enforce his just claims.

In the same way there is a belief current among the public that it is of no use to fight any Government Department for the redress of an injustice, for—rightly or wrongly—it is believed that, with the powerful legal machinery at its command, it can enforce its claims through every successive Court of Law, which procedure entails such expenditure that the ordinary citizen shrinks from the labour and the expense implied, even though he be fully convinced of the justice and truthfulness of his claims and assertions.

Now it must be admitted that the prevalence of such a belief affecting the attitude of the governed towards the government undermines the very spirit of democratic institutions, as these rest upon justice and truthfulness. A more subtle sphere in administrative activity, demanding nicer moral distinctions, is presented by the practice of the Departments I have here selected in ascertaining the taxable obligations of citizens, namely, in using indirect and not open sources of information, even such as might come under the heading of spying. Now we must admit that in all criminal investigation and procedure, or even where there is ground for *prima facie* suspicion, the employment of such means as come under the heading of detective work is admissible; but I maintain that when such primary grounds are not evident, and when the other party in the transaction is not clearly informed of a state of warfare, such action is distinctly reprehensible. It savours of underhandedness and untruthfulness and is essentially opposed to the leading national quality of the British people, namely, fair-play. Nay, even to use and thereby to encourage the activity of the unprofessional informer, before just grounds of criminal procedure or even of the suspicion of criminal practice have been established, savours of untruthfulness and dishonesty in dealing. By similar actions or traditions the government as such is sinning against its duty to Truth and, whatever material advantages may be gained, it is seriously under-

mining the moral health of the nation and destroying the
spirit of democracy.

Libel and Privilege.

The same applies to that group of public
activities which come under the law of libel
and confer certain immunities on what are
called "privileged statements."

In the light of the important subject with which we are
here dealing, the principles and practice of the law of libel
and slander in England are defective. The practice of the
English libel law is, *de jure* and *de facto*, a denial of our thesis
that truth is an actual asset to civilised society. For in this
law and its practice the contravention of truth only becomes
a real factor when "material damage" directly results from
it[1]. It is on this ground, and this ground only, that the law
takes cognisance of it. While, no doubt, the importance of
truth is admitted or implied, it in no way becomes the central element of legal importance or practical procedure. In
so far, truth, as such, is disregarded as a matter of supreme
importance in national life worthy of legislation to safe-
guard and to advance it; just as the idea of Honour (though
not wholly ignored) is not directly and prominently recognised as worthy of protection in such legislation.

In this respect English law differs in practice essentially
from French law. French law covering libel and slander[2]
summarises both these forms in the term *diffamation*. It
distinguishes between *diffamation* and *injure*. "Every alle-
gation or imputation of a fact which injures the honour of
any person, or the consideration in which such person is

---

[1] The common saying, "the greater the truth the greater the
libel" may contain an inaccurate epigrammatic exaggeration; but it
illustrates the point we wish to emphasise.

[2] See *Code d'Instruction Criminelle et Code Pénal*, 1913, pp. 600 seq.

held, or of the corporate body to whom the fact is imputed, is a *diffamation.*" ("*Toute allégation ou imputation d'un fait qui porte atteinte à l'honneur ou à la considération de la personne ou du corps auquel le fait est imputé est une diffamation.*") "Every insulting expression, term of contempt or invective which does not include the imputation of a definite fact, is an insult—*injure.*" ("*Toute expression outrageante, terme de mépris ou invective qui ne renferme l'imputation d'aucun fait est une injure.*")

There is thus an essential difference established in French law between the statement or implication of a definite action or fact on the one hand, which constitutes *diffamation*, and a general insult or invective which does not impute any definite fact or action, and constitutes *une injure*. In English law there is a definite distinction between slander and libel, determined by the form of publication. "A defamatory statement is a statement concerning any person which exposes him to hatred, ridicule or contempt, or which causes him to be shunned or avoided, or which has a tendency to injure him in his office, profession or trade. Such statement, if in writing, printing or other permanent form, is a libel; if in spoken words or significant gestures, a slander[1]."

A libel is always a more serious offence "because the law assumes that in case of libel, i.e. where the defamatory statement is in writing, printing or other permanent form, the person defamed has of necessity suffered damage, and is therefore entitled to maintain an action." On the other hand, in the case of slander, "...the plaintiff cannot succeed without proof of special damage, except in four cases. These four cases are: (1) where the words charged the plaintiff with

[1] See Sir Hugh Fraser's *Principles and Practices of the Law of Libel and Slander*, 5th Edition, 1917, p. 1.

having committed a criminal offence which is punishable corporally; or (2) where they impute that he has a contagious disease of a particular kind; or (3) where they are spoken of him in relation to his office, profession or trade; or (4) where they impute unchastity or adultery to any woman or girl" (Fraser, *Ibid.* pp. 32 seq.). "Thus a man may be called a cheat, rogue, swindler or villain, he may be charged with being immoral or profligate, unless such accusation relates to his conduct in office, profession or trade, or is connected with the duties of his office or profession, no action will lie. In order to make good his claim he must prove definite temporal loss, as for instance, loss of a client or customer, or loss or refusal of some appointment or employment; of a gift, pecuniary or otherwise, even though it be only gratui-tous hospitality—at dinner. The loss of a marriage may also be adduced; but not the strained relations and the prob-ability of a divorce in matrimony; nor the loss of friends, nor the possibility of actual damage, nor mental pain or distress, nor bodily illness, nor even expulsion from a re-ligious society. Even the future effect of such a slander, though producing no special damage (such as the loss of a directorate unless he can clear himself), will stand."

Now, whereas the idea of honour forms the central element in the conception in French libel and slander and whereas an insult as such is a punishable offence, the English law does not consider or admit such a conception as in itself establish-ing a *tort* or ground for a criminal action. The law only offers its protection where material damage can be proved.

No doubt the truth or untruth of a statement is admitted as of importance and as affecting "justification." But it is a most characteristic and instructive point to consider the ground upon which truth thus establishes "justification."

It is not on the ground of the moral outrage caused by the untruth, or of the absolute necessity of upholding truth both in law and morality, but because "the law will not permit a man to recover damages in respect of an injury to a character which he either does not or ought not to possess" (Fraser, *Ibid.* p. 145).

It will therefore be seen that some form of material injury which can be translated into definite material loss or gain constitutes a *tort* or crime. In no way does the law here confirm the importance of truth and honour and the criminality of offences against either.

Thus the principles and practices of the English law of libel and slander are indirectly destructive of the establishment and the safeguarding of truth in English life.

Privilege.   In some ways still more fatal to the spirit of truth are the limitations governing the law of libel and slander under the heading of "privileged statements." In certain cases, even though the matter complained of is defamatory, it is supposed to be in the interests of public policy that no liability attaches to the publication thereof. The occasion is privileged. These occasions are either of "absolute privilege" or of "qualified privilege." In the case of "absolute privilege" no action lies, "however untrue and malicious the statements may have been"; in the case of "qualified privilege" a statement made upon an occasion of this kind is *prima facie* protected. But proof of actual malice will, however, rebut the *prima facie* protection afforded by such an occasion. Moreover it is for the plaintiff (the libelled person) to prove that the defendant acted in bad faith, and not for the defendant to prove that he acted in good faith. It will readily be seen how difficult it is to establish legal proof of "malice." This privilege is granted to Members of Parliament speaking in Parliament, to judges and lawyers in their judicial functions, to Government officials, even to those of local governmental bodies, and to other corporate officials in their official capacity.

Now it will readily be perceived how it would hamper the political representatives in their public work and in the public interest, judges and lawyers who endeavour to carry out the law—in fact, officials of all kinds in the performance of their public or official duties—if they were constantly hampered or threatened by legal proceedings instituted to extort material compensation for damage done by innumerable people in work which, naturally dealing with the public, must or may offend a large number of individuals. On the other hand it must also be admitted that such privilege carries in itself a great tendency, if not a direct inducement to the ready and frequent commission of offences against the honour and interests of law-abiding citizens, and to the encouragement of untruth in its gravest and most effective form.

We must realise that it is possible for any Member of Parliament, judicial officer, pleading lawyer—even a member of a local corporation—to vent his personal spite and to injure, in the most vital part of his honour and reputation, whomsoever he may personally dislike or disapprove of. At all events it is possible for him thus to act without let or hindrance and rashly to make statements impugning the honour of others, while knowing that no punishment of the law will reach him, even if his statements are untrue or ill-founded, and even if they are made with malicious intent. It is true that some other Member of the House (if the statement be made there) may traverse such a statement and uphold the truth; but such rectification is left to the accident whether such an advocate of truth be forthcoming or not, the presumption being that there is no abundance of men prepared to oppose their colleagues in the interest of abstract morality.

Surely the public ought to be furnished with facile, prompt and effectively public means of an inexpensive character to refute such an untruth and confirm truth, not only in their own interest, but in the wider interest of a moral Society. It is in this direction that reforms are urgently needed, and in spite of the complexities of legal procedure could readily be initiated.

Besides these more definite sources of danger, there are other conditions in the life of modern democracies which are unfavourable to the prevalence of truth.

Autocracy has ever been the enemy of truth because it does not rest upon the moral sanction of Society, but upon an extra-social authority which is confirmed in its unquestioned irrational sway by the claims of a supernatural origin. In modern times the type of such an autocracy has been the Russian Tsardom. But contemporary history has shown how extremes may meet. For Russia is now enslaved by another autocracy, the Mob-Autocracy of the Bolsheviks. Though the Russian Tsardom was governed in its foreign as well as in its domestic policy by a bureaucracy merely aiming at the increase of conquests and of power, against the relentless advance of which even the Tsar himself was powerless, the lurid picture of the political rule of the late Tsar was at least relieved in its tenebrous maleficence by his action in initiating the Hague Peace Conference, and his splendid, almost heroic and drastic suppression of drink which was the central material cause of the physical and moral degradation

of his people. The Bolsheviks, it is true, began their career
by the pronouncement of the higher moral and political
principles in opposing annexation and in upholding the
principle of self-determination for the peoples of the world.
In so far they may have anticipated the powerful pronouncement of the leading principles for the national and international guidance of the world as put in a lasting and classic
form by President Wilson. But they have since then denied,
both in principle and practice, the moral grounds upon which
their revolution rested. They have substituted for the
abolition of international war the initiation of class war
throughout the world; and, while proclaiming the moral
and political rights of labour and of the labourers (to which
practically all citizens in every country belong), they are
endeavouring to establish the tyranny of one group of
labourers—those of the hand—over all other groups,
especially those who labour with the head. They are on
their part endeavouring to establish the rule of force in its
most brutal and degrading form, thereby denying the whole
moral evolution of the world throughout the ages.

Leaving these two forms of autocracy and tyranny—
Tsardom and Bolshevism—if we now turn to the modern
democracies, we find that, before the war and since the war,
the establishment of the rule of truth has been endangered
by three groups of forces, which the economic and social
evolution of the modern conditions of life have produced
among us, and whose influence can be traced to the detriment of the prevalence of truth which we wish to see
established in every one of our civilised and democratic
nations. These three forces can be identified with the
Politician, the Millionaire, and the Journalist.

CHAPTER IV.

THE POLITICIAN

THE modern politician tends to become the journalist in action. The power of ready formulation and of ready and emphatic enunciation, coupled with the manipulative skill in directing the machinery of public life, is more and more likely to become the decisive factor of success as it also absorbs most of the thought and energy of the successful politician. Thus the means of government tend to over-shadow and to absorb the end of government, as the party machine and its efficient working in itself, as well as the repair of its internal construction, absorb the attention to the exclusion of the great work which the machine itself has to do[1]. This applies as well to the definite departmental work in government (with which I have dealt above) as it does to the ultimate social and moral ends of governing a nation for its own welfare and for the good of a wider humanity beyond it. While thus there have been but few statesmen in modern times whose knowledge of specific departments in public life was outstanding, there have been still fewer in the immediate past whose political activity was directed and inspired by wider ideals of national and humanitarian progress. Whatever criticisms may be urged against many aspects and incidents in the political career of the two great leaders of British politics in the last generation, Disraeli and Gladstone, it must be conceded that they stand out on the horizon line of European politics as having

[1] See *Patriotism, National and International*, Chap. v. pp. 87 seq.

been actuated by great and insistent ultimate ideals, the influence of which can be traced in almost every one of their definite policies, as it also inspired and illumined their stupendous energy and work and was undoubtedly the determining factor in their influence upon the mass of the people, and their practical success as leaders of men. With Disraeli, these ideals were those of a largely conceived imperialism, as the realisation of the destiny of the historical life of the English people; and the growth in power of this British Empire was in no way to be divorced from the elevation in prospect and in tone of British national life, still less from the happiness and advancement of humanity at large. The thrilling watchword and piercing beacon-light in the political and private life of Gladstone was the Cause of Liberty coupled with tolerance—both liberty and tolerance fused into an active and dominating Christianity. This Christianity was literally conceived as the Christianity of the Anglican Church, which might unite with, but should transfuse and dominate all other forms of Christian worship, as it would inspire and direct the moral character of all the people of the earth to the improvement and elevation of their lives. Whatever compromise may have been made in the realisation of these great ideals by these two statesmen —consciously, or subconsciously—the permeating presence in their public and their private life and the modification of their lives and their activity by these ideals are undeniable.

It is difficult to find the right focus for visualising public men in the immediate present, standing, as we necessarily do, so close to them. Several, if not all of them, are undoubtedly men of moral integrity and have high ideals of life. Moreover this tragic war has stirred the nations as well as the statesmen to formulate the national aims at their highest and to bring them into direct relation with the ideals of civilised humanity. Every exponent of the national will of the Allies has risen to this high task of statesmanship, culminating in the monumental pronouncements of American War Aims by President Wilson.

But with this admission, which might, no doubt, be extended to several other modern statesmen, the fact still remains that the absorption of the end of government into the means of governing and its machinery, is so great, that even these leaders have often deliberately turned, or involuntarily drifted, from the road which leads to the highest democratic form of government to the tortuous by-paths of party management and political trickery; furthermore that their knowledge of the facts of economic, social and political life was incomplete, often superficial and characterised by both haste and opportunism—in one word that they were wanting in the strong and refined sense of truth, as we have hitherto endeavoured to define it, and that their actions were not guided and permeated by it. In consequence the power of those who are really in possession of the knowledge and the skill to perform the definite tasks which public life imposes, is, by our political system, weakened, if not entirely dissolved, while still less effectiveness can, through this, be given to the endeavours of those whose maturity of thought and singleness of purpose lead them to devote themselves to the realisation of the ideals which are truly and adequately expressive of the best that is in us and in our age.

Whatever the untold misery caused by this war may be, the personal grief and loss which it has brought to millions of people in every part of the civilised world, the destruction of the best manhood, physical and moral, in each of the nations, the absolute annihilation of treasure and the material impoverishment of the whole world, the demoralisation of mankind as regards its valuation of human life and the conduct of life as regards human fraternity and love as well as honourable and truthful dealings with all men—in spite of all these losses, among the compensations in self-sacrifice and heroism and many heroic virtues which it has evoked, one of the most valuable and—let us hope—most lasting results in the political life of civilised nations will be, that, more especially through the official pronouncements of President Wilson, the political aims and ideals of modern democracy, at once lofty and practical, have been formulated with unassailable clearness and decision. Whatever history may decide as to President Wilson's responsibility for the lateness of the date at which the United States entered the war—(which, had it been earlier, might have led to a more speedy termination of the conflict)—he will stand forth in all ages as having followed the traditions of Washington and Lincoln who forced great moral issues, as the determining factors, into national and international politics, so that these moral factors can no longer be ignored—and have now in fact for all belligerents become the conscious aims for which the nations are fighting[1]. Nor, as regards the special subject with which we are here dealing, must we forget that, in one of his subsequent messages to Congress, he announced that "The Russians were poisoned by the same falsehoods which kept the German people in the dark. The only antidote is the truth."

It rests with us to see that after the war this raising of the platform of national and international politics is not succeeded by a period of relapse into the lower strata of party politics and of cynical contest to uphold separate interests,

[1] See *Patriotism, National and International*, II. pp. 3 seq.

and that there is no reaction into the political repudiation of our moral standards caused by a just denial and resentment of Pacifist Inopportunism, Bolshevik ineptitude or treachery or Socialist substitution of class-rivalry and economic tyranny for the higher social and moral aspirations, national as well as international. For, unfortunately, the leading principles of higher social and international morality have been arrogated to themselves, and been disfigured and caricatured, by these three political factions during the war itself; and the natural antagonism against these bodies may include and carry with it a reaction against the ideas and ideals in no sense theirs, but emphatically belonging to all right-thinking men who have fought this war in order to uphold them[1].

[1] I cannot resist giving in full a letter written by a soldier at the front and published in *The Spectator* of Jan. 26, 1918, which forcibly impresses our duty for the future. "The domestic political situation in Great Britain is obscure and depressing. The flower of the population is fighting, and the weeds are scrambling for money and power. Agitators and self-assertive little men have produced a war-weariness in this country which at times looks like black treason to the men in the trenches. Submarines have diminished our food supplies; aeroplanes have bombed London. These are as trifles to the sufferings which a soldier bears during one hour of battle; but the faint-hearts groan and grow weary, and the Yellow Press, prostituting itself for an increased circulation, gives words to the feelings of the poltroons. They clamour for new Ministers, new Admirals, more bread and more cinemas. The self-sacrificing idealism, the imagination needed to picture to themselves what is at stake, they lack. Who will stimulate them to it? Not Mr Lloyd George, whose oratory is fine but whose reliability they rightly doubt. Not the Church, whose leaders still speak in the language of the classics to those who better understand the language of Billingsgate. Not Sir Arthur Yapp, whose tongue tries to do what his hands cannot. Not the soldiers, for they have lost all patience and can no longer persuade, but must abuse if they speak at all. Any man who would claim to be a statesman now must soon lift up his voice and tell these people that it is not their wretched

It is not unlikely that the contest among the parties in
each State and among the nations, in the immediate future,
will centre round the question of moral principles and their
effective guidance of national and international politics--

homes, nor their miserable daily wage, nor the bread with which they
fill their flabby bellies for which millions of men have laid down their
lives. It is a great and high ideal of freedom and peace for which we
are fighting, and, if we lose the war, life will not be worth living even
if we have food for our stomachs and palaces to live in. Let it not
be thought that all the people in these islands are of this wretched
way of thinking. It is only the clamorous few. The great mass of
the people are working hard for victory, but they also hardly know
what victory or defeat means. They lack imagination; they have
not seen great cities in ruins, women violated, children crucified.
They see only through a glass darkly what the people of France and
Belgium have seen face to face, and they are only too ready to be
'led' by any so-called 'leader' who may arise among them. Such
'leaders' usually appeal to the mere material wants of their hearers;
they are usually men of a narrow class outlook, whose 'world' is at
its largest England, and at its smallest the industrial centre in which
they live. What is needed is a real leader of Labour, a man who can
combine his interest in the working man with an interest in and
intelligent perception of world-politics, a man who will sink the so-
called 'class-war' in the greater issue of the world-war by teaching
the people how the Allies are fighting that very battle against a
ruling military *class*, which should appeal to every democrat the
world over. Such a man must be ready to impress on his hearers the
need for sacrifice at home and the need for thrift. This need will be
felt after the war, and the men and women who have squandered
large wages will regret their folly: these very people have now in their
hands the means of producing more 'social reform' than a dozen
Acts of Parliament can procure them. They could have good houses,
good boots and good food, and set aside a sum for their old age, at
the same time lending it to their country. Yet too many are simply
throwing away their money on cheap jewellery, pianos that they
cannot play, and drink. Social reform must come from below, and
no Act of Parliament can succeed unless the people set themselves
to improve their own homes. What is our education doing? If it is
not teaching it is useless. One thing stands out as certain amid all
the pessimism of people who are too concerned with the smaller

the clash between class-interests, the interests of occupations pronounced to be sufficient grounds for party differences and conflicts by the "practical men," and the insistence upon the guidance and determination of such interests by higher moral and social ideas and ideals by those who claim the subordination of political and economic interests to moral needs and aspirations. There will be also extreme Nationalists and Internationalists in foreign politics. Perhaps the first political contest will be waged on the question of the equitable distribution of economic opportunity among nations[1]; and here the cleavage will be the support or the denial of the moral and equitable factor which each party will give.

In any case we may hope that the politician of the future will, by the weight of historic events, be forced to consider, and to be actively guided by, the higher moral factors and aims in the life of each nation and of civilised humanity.

material issues in life. If we as a people preserve the will to win, and exercise the energy and endurance which the soldiers in France are proving to be the great inheritance of the British race, we can and we shall win the war. If we can get back at least some of the high enthusiasm and idealism of 1914, we shall also win the peace which will follow it. But if we sacrifice the blood and treasure of this Empire for a mere return to the *status quo ante*, then England, though great to all outward appearance and victorious in battle, will never again be a great nation among the nations of the world. We must take into our hearts the high aspirations and noble ideals of those who have fought in the line and of those who have died. They did not fight for wealth or for comfort, but for truth and for justice, for the defence of the weak against the oppression of the strong, and for the destruction of the old ideas which have brought forth war. War may not be destroyed for ever by this war, but it will have received a staggering blow. The subsequent peace in course of time may banish it for ever from the earth."

[1] See Preface to the American edition of *Aristodemocracy*, etc.

In these deficiencies of the State, however, there is one redeeming and consoling factor which is absent in the cases of the millionaire and the journalist. The politician is removable, and it lies legally and directly within the power of the democracy to change and replace him by another, if he has been unsuccessful or has acted reprehensibly. It is not so in the case of the millionaire and the journalist.

CHAPTER V.

THE MILLIONAIRE

THE millionaire may be assassinated by a criminal, whose motives are those of personal vindictiveness, or by a wrong-headed fanatic. But such isolated and reprehensible removals of a single millionaire in no way alter the system by which stupendous power is given to individuals without any public or private responsibility. I am not referring to the financial and commercial control placed in the hands of the millionaire by the accretion of great wealth, growing in proportion with this increase, which very accretion favours the growth of his power[1]; but I am considering the moral (in many cases distinctly immoral) social and political power given to these men even in spheres most remote from the direct increase of wealth. Such men are often endowed with power equal to that of the State, in many cases surpassing it, to create or to modify moral and social institutions, religious movements and all that makes for national education. They can found new institutions, encourage or discourage social organisations, charities and educational bodies. As their encouragement is directly effective, so too is their discouragement. It will readily be seen how the actions of those in charge of such institutions, depending upon voluntary contributions to their funds, will be affected by the

[1] I have dwelt elsewhere upon this *irresponsible* power of the millionaire as being contrary to "good policy." See *The Political Confession of a Practical Idealist*, London (John Murray), 1911, pp. 22 seq.; *Aristodemocracy*, etc., Appendix IV. pp. 382—395.

granting of large contributions or the withholding of the same. Such individual financial autocrats may have it in their power to impress the stamp of their own immature or distorted intellectual conceptions of what the immediate and ultimate preparation for life ought to be upon the educational system and character of a whole nation or a whole age. Though these men may sometimes be actuated by high and unselfish aims, their own intellectual education and aspirations may be far below the level of the average society in which they live. It is even probable that the bias which their successful business career,—continuous and all-absorbing in its concentration upon one not too lofty aim,—may give to their mentality, definitely unfits them for the apprehension of the moral and intellectual aims of education. No doubt these men are able to seek and to find the advice of trustworthy experts to guide them in their excursions into the field of public education. There have indeed been instances in which their interference has been distinctly salutary and beneficent. But there are innumerable cases in which—though they have not encouraged what is manifestly bad or useless—yet the discouragement of studies not appealing to their materialistic minds, and the narrow directions in which their benefactions have been most effective, have entirely altered the due proportion and relationship of the several departments of intellectual and moral training within the community and have—to use medical terms—produced atrophy on the one side and hypertrophy on the other. The result would be, that, if their interventions and schemes were to prevail over all others without restriction, the whole mentality of a nation or of an age might be distorted or vitiated. To say the least: the successful financier is not an expert in educational matters, and if his pronouncements are made and accepted as thorough and as final, the result is a lie. What is still more important is that this power for harm is entirely an irresponsible one and that the evil-doer or bungler in matters of such great public concern is irremovable.

The Newspaper Proprietor[1].

Such a millionaire may buy, and often has bought up, a newspaper. To all intents and purposes he thus becomes a journalist or, at all events, one who wields journalistic power

---

[1] Since this book was written a discussion has taken place in the House of Commons as to the admissibility of proprietors of newspapers to Government office. My own opinion on this question is, that proprietors and editors of newspapers—the journalists—are as eligible to represent the country in Parliament and to hold office as are the representatives of any other profession or business. Indeed, it appears to me that, if they directly advise the public as to the settlement of matters of State, upholding definite policies or views, they should do this as manifest advocates of views they hold, so that they can be personally identified with their published opinions and, above all, made responsible for their utterances and propaganda. Moreover it will then be possible for the public either to confirm them in power or to remove them from office and from their seat in Parliament. At present they may exercise power as great, or even greater than, that of any member of the Government, hidden behind the journalistic machinery, personally unidentified and in no way responsible for the policy they uphold—moreover irremovable from their own seat of hidden power. Furthermore, as in the case of any business or professional man who resigns his business connexions when entering the Government, they ought conscientiously and effectively to sever all connexion with the newspapers in which they have been interested and in no way use them, directly or indirectly, to enforce their own opinions. It may be impracticable to enact a law that a newspaper proprietor or journalist should not use his own press-organ in support of his candidature for Parliament during an election: but at least a custom ought to be established, in conformity with the English-speaking tradition of fair-play and fair fighting, that one of the contestants should not use arms of which his opponent is deprived.

Since the above was written an interview with Lord Northcliffe

in the most effective form. As a matter of fact, not only the individual millionaire, but groups of financial interests, large financial corporations and Stock Exchange manipulators, do control newspapers. In many cases this is freely admitted and accepted by public opinion; and it will be said in some countries that one paper is owned by a certain group of financial or industrial interests, a second by another. The power of the great armament firms wielded through journalistic channels has been frequently exposed and commented upon. They control, not only newspapers in their own country, but even in the countries of their prospective allies or enemies, the news in which is distinctly coloured by the red glare of war. In a less direct way, not as the owners of the newspaper, but as those who possess certain degrees of power over them, large industrial and commercial concerns, whose business depends to a great extent upon profuse advertising, may claim and receive important concessions in

(who had taken charge of an important department of War Propaganda under the Government) has been published in the press of April 27, 1918:

"Lord Northcliffe replying to a telephone inquiry yesterday, stated that while he has protested publicly and privately against the recent weakening of the War Cabinet, he has agreed, at the request of the Prime Minister, and other members of the Cabinet to continue the difficult and delicate work in which he is engaged until the Government can find someone else to carry on his tasks. He is in no sense a member of the Government, and has declined to become one, in order that his newspapers may be free to speak plainly about certain aspects of the political and military situation."

It will be seen that a newspaper proprietor, whose several newspapers are of exceptional power in directly forming or influencing public opinion in accordance with his personal opinions, accepts direct official work under the Government, yet surprisingly—or at least with astonishing naïveté—refuses to become responsible for these opinions to the public in the ordinary system of political responsibility adopted by all democratic countries.

the distribution of news and the expression of opinion, even among the leading newspapers. I remember an instance in the United States, when I was informed that a certain matter would, if desired, be kept out of the papers by the intervention of a friendly proprietor of a great department-store, whose requests were, by implication or by direct threat, backed by the power of withholding his costly advertisements from such a paper.

In many cases, however, the millionaire and even the financial corporations who control the newspapers, do not concentrate their influence on the editing of them for the furtherance of their definite business interests, but extend their arbitrary power in asserting their personal opinions or hobbies, which, without clearly indicating to the public any trace of origin and authority, may thus force upon the world, by the privilege of this form of monopoly in publicity, their own predilection, prejudices or antagonisms. There are even cases, far from infrequent, in which the personal preferences, animosities or capricious likes or dislikes of such financial potentates concerning public men and even private individuals, are directly manifested and made efficient in the most powerful form of publicity, without any possibility of self-defence on the part of the victim. All public men know what "a good press" or "a bad press" means. The acts and public pronouncements, occasional speeches as well as publications, of statesmen, public servants, authors and artists, can receive full or very meagre attention, fair or unfair, favourable or unfavourable notices, and this may be decided, not only by the political or acknowledged bias of the paper, or even by the personal bias of the editor and his staff, but by the personal malevolence or caprice of the proprietor. There are undeniable cases in which the proprietors of news-

papers have directly used their journalistic organ to repri-
mand and to injure in the lighter social sphere of life people
of whose actions and personalities they disapproved. I was
credibly informed some years ago by the sub-editor of a
paper, that in their office there existed for consultation a
Black List, provided for their use by the proprietor, which
contained the names of all persons of whom he had reason
to disapprove and whose names were never to be mentioned
in his newspaper; and that this ostracism even extended to
the members of their families. Whether they made speeches
or wrote books, whether they or their wives or daughters
opened bazaars or were present at social gatherings, their
names were not to appear in his paper. Such petty use of
power is perhaps unimportant and not worthy of consideration. But it certainly does not uphold the standard of
Truth, and gives power of evil-doing and of annoying one's
neighbour—not to consider at all the grosser criminal or
quasi-criminal forms of blackmail, resorted to by practically
criminal proprietors of the lower kinds of newspapers—not
only to the proprietor and editor, but to every member of
the staff, down to the lowest and most illiterate reporter of
scraps of news. All this lowers the standard of veracity and
general morality in the community, and may cause grave
harm or unmerited annoyance, as in most cases it cannot be
redressed or remedied.

So far, I have merely dealt with the clearly condemnable
developments of irresponsible power in the hands of the
newspaper proprietors. Now, there is no doubt that many
of these men are not actuated by any lower motives of this
kind. They may even be wise, good, patriotic and public-
spirited men. It can safely be asserted that, though there
has been a steady degeneration of character and tone in

English journalism within the last thirty years, the newspapers of Great Britain have kept a comparatively high level of integrity and freedom from directly personal interference on the part of their proprietors. On several occasions where these did interfere, they did so—at least conscientiously and professedly—from patriotic motives. In some cases this interference may have been both timely and useful; in others, it has been the reverse. The more effective it has been, however, the more dangerous is the establishment of a tradition in which any individual, not directly responsible to the public for his public acts, can use the stupendous and unique power which the possession of the monopoly of publicity gives, without redress, without granting to his opponents an equal power of bringing home to the public the opposing news in the same emphatic and effective medium, and without the power vested in the democracy of deposing the holder of such national machinery of public influence from his position. If any man, through the accidental possession of this monopoly (accidental as far as the expression of the public will is concerned) becomes the mouthpiece of the nation's opinion and the leader and guide of the public will, he ought to be called on to form a government and to be subject to all the responsibilities of his high office. Every word and every action of his ought thus to be clearly identified with him personally, be open to criticism and censure, and he ought to be removable from the spheres of public influence should the nation disapprove of his action. As it is, whatever happens, whether his predictions as well as his statements have been discredited, the direct power of influencing public opinion, as far as the machinery of publicity is concerned, remains intact in his hands.

The abuses and the evil influence exercised through these

channels of newspaper publicity are not only or chiefly confined to the accident of power placed in the hands of a corrupt, unfair or injudicious newspaper proprietor, they are essential to the very nature of the newspaper itself in the development of modern journalism. They are influential in producing the type of the modern journalist, from the editor to the humblest reporter as he has been evolved by the modern newspaper itself, and are effective in the education of the journalist and the conception of his career even in its highest form. What, above all, concerns us here is the effect of journalism in lowering and demoralising the central factor in public morality, namely, the sense of Truth.

CHAPTER VI.

THE PROFESSIONAL JOURNALIST

THE dominating and all-absorbing object in the purveying of news, over-riding all other aims—in fact ignoring and brushing them aside when they obstruct—is to provide the earliest news, the most sensational news, in the most sensational form, which will arrest the attention of the reader. Even if there be no ulterior and more reprehensible object in the management of a newspaper such as we have indicated above, and even if the interests of one or other of the political parties do not modify the selection, distribution and presentation of news, these aims are nevertheless the dominating and guiding principles of successful journalism.

I am ignoring those flagrant and manifestly criminal cases which unfortunately abound, in which false news is deliberately spread.

Priority of Publication. But it is evident that in this race for priority in publication the careful weighing and testing of facts in order to ensure Truth are impossible, and that haste of statement is not only not conducive to the establishment of Truth, but that it is a factor which itself undermines the moral and intellectual quality of thoroughness essential to a truth-loving nature. The man whose mentality is absorbingly and habitually filled with the one desire of haste in statement, is not likely to develop a conscientious striving after Truth. On the contrary he is in all probability bound to blunt his fine sense of this cardinal virtue. Now the competition between the several newspapers to be first in the publication of any news is so keen, that it has often led to the gravest injuries to the public interest and even to tragic pain to large numbers of individuals. Who, for instance, can forget the misery caused to many a family when the false news was spread that the British Legation at Pekin, besieged by the Chinese, had fallen into the enemy's hands and all the men, women and children who had sought refuge there, had probably been murdered?

Selection of News. Sensationalism. Next to the priority in the distribution of news comes the selection of the most sensational news. In no way do I wish to limit selection in the choice of news, which, on the face of it, is of deep concern and most directly touches the interests of the large mass of the people. The test for such selection is to be found in what in one phrase we should call Public Concern. The values are set by the relative importance of news. But the choice is in many, if not in most, cases actually determined by the startling character of the news which forcibly arrests attention, irrespective of its conforming to the interests of the public; it is not determined by its true intrinsic importance. It thus becomes sensational. In the relative proportion of things which concern the life of a nation, the facts are exaggerated and distorted and in so far falsified.

Obtrusion of the Personal Side of Life. Still more is this the case when the personal and private concerns of people's lives are grotesquely treated as matters of national importance and obtruded upon public notice, merely to gratify the morbid or vulgar curiosity of our lower instincts. Even if they do not come within the pale of what is technically called slander or libel, they respond to this

lower tendency in human nature which they habitually encourage—itself, as we have seen above, destructive of the
sense of Truth.

If these strictures are justified with regard to
Journalistic the selection and distribution of facts, they
Form and
Style. still more emphatically apply to the literary
form in which they are presented to the public.
I am not referring to the sensational headlines which have
come into vogue within the last generation. Much can be
urged in their favour on the ground of convenience, in en-
abling the reader systematically and rapidly to scan the
paper for the news in which he is concerned and which
interests him. But this supreme aim of arresting attention
goes far beyond the headlines and permeates all forms of
exposition and composition in journalistic writing. I am not
even considering the supremely grotesque and vulgar
literary solecisms to which the compressed headlines in
many newspapers lead. But even in the more temperate
and superior editing of our leading papers, sensational exaggeration in form and diction is day by day encroaching
upon the rule of veracity as well as of good taste. The
ultimate goal that apparently is being thus approached in
journalistic style is the standard of the advertising agent—
as no doubt this important factor in newspaper management
does exert the most potent influence in the evolution of
modern journalism. The one aim is to catch the eye and to
arrest attention. I venture to believe that one of the leading
characteristics of the literary mentality and style of our age
may hereafter be considered the rule of exaggerated diction
and of humorous paradox; as on the negative side it has led
to the horror of the platitude, a sneering attribute often
applied to Truth. Even in the literary character of our

leading writers, some of whom may win a permanent place in English literature, together with many remarkable and outstanding qualities, we may discover this modern taint of exaggeration in diction, over-emphasis leading to coarseness, humour to cynicism and paradox blunting veracity. In any case, our literature has been infected by the " Journalese."

Effect on the Reading Public. If this is the effect upon the literary world, the cumulative effect upon the wider reading public is still more disastrous as regards the refinement of taste and veracity. And when we consider that perhaps three-quarters—it may even be nine-tenths—of the reading of the civilised world is confined to the daily newspapers, their influence upon moral and intellectual mentality, especially on that side of it which interests us here, can readily be gauged.

CHAPTER VII.

THE IDEAL JOURNALIST

Such being the character and essential nature of newspapers, with their main objects and ideals, it follows that the profession of the modern journalist has developed into the wrong channels and that, from the nature of his career, and even the system of his education and preparation, his activity is not conducive to the development of a high sense of Truth—in fact that it is all wrong. I will forbear to exhibit the lowest form of the blackmailing "penny-a-liner" and of the self-seeking *Streber* with low or distorted ideals, who stand self-condemned before all right-minded people. Yet we must remember that their power of public evil and of private spite is infinitely raised by their association with this monopolised form of general publicity; and that even men and women of high standing and eminence are powerless against their machinations. I will confine myself to the very highest forms of the journalistic type, men who themselves have the loftiest conception of their profession and their duties. Their education and career encourage superficial knowledge, the hasty adoption of decided views, exaggerated diction, and the appeal to passion and prejudice or unjustifiable curiosity on the part of the reading public—all of which is directly opposed to our conception of Truth.

I recall with pleasure a striking conversation which I had more than twenty years ago in a foreign capital with one of the best types of modern journalists. He was then in the early stages of his eminently successful career, intensely

keen as regards the work and outlook of his profession, full
of enthusiasm for the good he was convinced it could do in
the world, and determined to carry into effect its best purpose and to uphold its highest ideals. He was determined to
persevere in fitting himself by arduous study and work in
the preparation for his special craft, and never to lose sight
of its higher ultimate aims. I do not know what exactly his
previous education was. I doubt whether he had the advantage of an academic education in one of the more prominent
universities, and whether there was any subject in which he
at any time received special and thorough training. In
watching his subsequent career, I must admit that he has
done remarkable work, some of it undeniably and eminently
good. But at the same time there is evidence of distinct
limitations in his horizon-line of vision, experience and
understanding. There is also evidence of distinct narrowness
and some leading prejudices, though there can be no doubt
of his ardent patriotism and his general longing for enlightenment.

He had listened patiently and attentively to my attack
upon his profession, especially on the ground of its encouraging superficiality of study and exposition, as compared
with the thorough training and the thorough work of the
specialist in science and learning, and of the evils resulting
from the effective diffusion of such imperfect knowledge.

"Ah," he said, "you forget that I am—or rather, that the
perfect journalist is—also a specialist. We journalists
specialise in one department of intellectual life, concentrate
our attention upon it, train every faculty to contribute to
this one task, by perseverance and self-abnegation to perfect
the thought-machine for the work it has to do, as much as
any of your scientific, historical, philosophic or artistic

specialists prepare themselves for their work. Our specialty is the rapid induction from the facts of life to meet the demands of, and to satisfy the need for, immediate information, which the pulsating rush of life claims, and rightly claims, as one of the essential requisites of its rational, intellectual as well as practical existence. The world cannot wait for the slow and deliberate elaboration of the material essential to life in the isolated study of your philosopher and scientist. Long before these have come to a conclusion and have deigned to present their results to an impatient world, the need for action has come and gone, and the public would be left without any guidance at all if it had depended upon them. Moreover, mark you, I have referred to the isolated study of the philosopher. The very qualities which go to the making of a true scientist and philosopher, the theoretic faculty, relegate him to the cloistered cell, the '*verfluchtes, dumpfes Mauerloch*' whence Faust broke forth to throw himself into the vortex of life. He need not be a complete recluse; but his training as well as his intellectual predisposition and the high objects of his work, probably, if not necessarily, exclude him from the rushing and palpitating life about him—he is out of touch with life. Meanwhile the public is clamouring for enlightenment and guidance, and it asks for this direct and at once. It is I who must give it. It is the rapidity of judgment, the almost automatic spontaneity in forming an opinion on the facts before me, the right instinct of setting the right values on such facts for the purposes and needs of the public whom I wish to enlighten, the whetting of the perceptions and, above all, of the reasoning powers, so that they may work unhampered by irrelevant or obstructive considerations which do not conduce to rapid judgment, so that in the shortest possible time, my thought-machine should produce the right conclusions. This faculty of the mind can itself be trained to such a high degree of working perfection that, compared with the same mental instruments of your recluse student, it works as the fingers of a trained virtuoso on a musical instrument can correctly give the scales, trills and quavers as well as the fuller chords, compared to the slow, stiff and bungling manipulation of even a great musical composer who has not practised the manipulation of the instrument. He cannot think rapidly; I can. I am training myself to do it. I have specialised in this great department of human knowledge—which is surely not without some importance. Will you deny me the right to do this? Will you think me arrogant and presumptuous if I claim to be a colleague and peer to your specialists of the noble House of the Mind? Is there not even some moral justification for my calling and some noble aspirations in following its clamorous appeal?

"Now, remember, that I have definite facts to deal with, to study, to hunt up, to dig for, quite apart from the art of expression, the literary power of persuasion and the adaptation of my style to reach the ears, to force and hold the attention of the confused and stolid mass of people called the Public. Here in the centre of this industrial, intellectual, political and international activity, I must constantly keep myself in touch with every manifestation of life, with every class and group of society, from the highest officials down to the hungry and humble labourer; I must suppress all social likings and prejudices, I must be friends with them all, hear what they have to say and balance the right and wrong of it, and then focus it in the light of the national interests of my country and the interests and the tastes of the public for whom my paper caters. Does this attitude of mind and the discipline it exacts not constitute a specialty? Could you or any of the truth-seekers you admire fulfil this task? Try it and let us see what will be the result! I have my work, you have yours. Yours may be better than mine. But there is need for my work in the world, and I mean to do it as well as I can."

CHAPTER VIII.

CRITICAL EXAMINATION OF THIS IDEAL OF JOURNALISM

My answer to him was then, and would be now, the following: "I take it that there are three main divisions in the preparation for, and the fulfilment of, the great and important task you have set yourself, not in any way severed from one another in your mind, but all working together, interpenetrating one another organically in your own mind for one great object. Though they are thus intended to be fused and united, it will help us to arrive at the truth in subdividing them and considering them first singly and then in their organic unity. There is, in the first place, the important task of getting at the facts, the information with which you have to deal. After that follows the forming of your judgment on these facts. And there is in the third place the exposition of these facts and judgments in a striking and emphatic form, which is again modified by what you consider to be the needs of the public for whom you cater.

News. "Let me at once concede that I do not quarrel with the first of these tasks, and that I admit the great utility. You will see, as we proceed, that I consider this the chief, if not the only, function of journalism in the literal meaning of that term, i.e. of ephemeral writing, of the *daily* newspaper. But even this paltry, and, no doubt, to your mind, grudging admission of mine I must limit, because of the very organic nature of the journalistic faculty as you have described it, and on account of which you might reasonably have opposed my sub-division of your work into three departments. It is just because the selection of these facts is directed by the totality of your individual mind, as you have described it, and is therefore coloured by your constitutional and dominant aim of the second and third requirements of the journalist, that I would even qualify and limit your absolute fitness for determining what are important and what are unimportant facts. Because you are to use the innumerable facts of life in order to form an immediate and rapid judgment; and, above all, because they are destined for a definite newspaper, with its own social and political bias and for a definite public, well- or ill- (generally ill) prepared critically to receive such judgment; and moreover, because you must be guided by the individual likings and intellectual interests (in no way including the love of Truth) of such a public; and, finally, because the form and style of imparting this knowledge would naturally partake of the nature of the emphatic, exaggerated, sensational and advertising character of modern journalism. For all these reasons, I do not think that your special training and mentality are best fitted truthfully and unerringly to convey news. Were the newspaper to be merely the *news' paper* the utility and justifiability of this your main function would be undeniable.

"Even as it is, this, the most important part of your professional work is not (or at all events ought not to be) confined to your craft. It ought to be one of the most important functions of our diplomatic staff. They ought to impose upon themselves the arduous duty of getting into touch, and remaining in touch, with the metropolis and the whole country to which they are accredited, and to the suppression of all their personal social bias and preferences. They ought to have on their staff—and as a matter of fact, most of them have—specialists who, while being men of the world, can also investigate commercial, industrial and financial facts and conditions as well as you can. Presumably even (for the fact that they have specialised on the study of these social phenomena does not put them at a disadvantage compared to you) they ought to select and to communicate these facts more efficiently than you can. I admit that these ideals in the staffing of our diplomatic corps are far from being realised; that, to the great detriment of national and international interests, their social intercourse is in many, if not in most, cases limited to definite sets which are far from being representative of the national, social and economic life of the country to which they are accredited[1]. You may perhaps rightly urge that the manifestly official position of the staff of an Embassy or Legation may preclude them from, or at least to some degree impede, their effective social blending with all classes of a community, and in so far be less favourable to the acquisition of facts which the ideal journalist can more readily get at. I have known cases among members of our own diplomatic service to whom this deficiency would certainly not apply. But there is no reason why—even without the hateful Secret Service of underhand spying—an embassy or a legation should not include employees possessing the qualifications which in this respect you claim for the journalist. If you or your colleagues possess such exceptional knowledge, why should you not impart it (as no doubt you often do) to the official quarters,

[1] It is highly probable, for instance, that the blunders which, to some degree, conduced to the grave and terrifically tragic event of the great European War were made by the German diplomatic representatives in England, who were more or less confined in their social intercourse to definite groups far from representative of the national will.

where it is most needed and where, presumably, the best use would be made of it? For remember—I really need not remind *you* of it—that your information is at once transmitted into the vortex of that haste and hurry, and often confusion, represented by the editorial departments of a great newspaper at night time; and that it is there entrusted to the tender mercies of a harassed sub-editor, who may or may not be well qualified wisely to select his news pouring in from all quarters. I remember your distinguished predecessor bitterly complaining to me how frequently the most important news and articles which he transmitted to your newspaper found their way into the wastepaper basket, and how often comparatively irrelevant messages were published with undue prominence. Even if there were not these fatal deficiencies, the great fact to which I have before alluded remains, that the judgment and bias of that individual newspaper itself, with all the possibilities of error and worse than error (after all, ultimately centered in one irresponsible individual), are not the best vehicle for transmitting even the truth about definite facts to a public hungering for information and enlightenment[1]. On the other hand, such information and such facts transmitted through diplomatic channels

---

[1] It has often occurred that the selection or emphasis given to news, the prominence or relegation to remote corners of the paper or the complete suppression of some news depends upon changes of editors. When enquiring of those who are acquainted with the internal business of newspapers, we have been answered: "Why, don't you know that the paper has changed hands? It now belongs to So-and-So who is keen on Protection or Free Trade, who hates the Scotch or the Jews." Or "this individual or group of people has now got a controlling interest"; or "this editor or sub-editor (who was an Oxford man) is replaced by another who is a Cambridge man," etc., etc. Such facts, quite unknown to the reading public, modify the character of a paper even in the selection and publication of news.

to a well-organised Foreign Office are there considered in relation to correlated information and facts from all other important centres and receive (or are supposed to receive) mature and due consideration by those entrusted with the national and international interests in which the public is concerned. Of course, the one postulate remains, and is now more clamorously called for than ever before in the world's history, namely, that the work of the Foreign Office in all free countries should be laid clearly before the public upon whom the ultimate decisions should rest in these matters as well as in home affairs; and that, if the public be not sufficiently trained to judge of such matters now, it ought to be one of the chief objects of the Foreign Office, *purely in the light of Truth*, to render these questions and problems intelligible to the average mind. I deliberately maintain that the facts with which foreign politics are concerned are, if anything, less complicated and less inaccessible to just apprehension than are most of the leading problems of economic and social life. Moreover, if the general public in a democracy is as yet not sufficiently trained in matters of international interest to approach and to grasp the problems of diplomacy, there is no reason why such training should not be given to them at once, in order to fit the mass of the electors for a task in which they are eminently concerned, and for the consummation of which they are ultimately responsible.

The Student of Economics, Politics and Sociology.
"I also readily admit to you that the student and philosopher, as you have described them in the classical figure of Faust, are, by their training and their actual mentality, not fitted to cope with the problems of life with which your journalist has to deal. But even in the literary type you have chosen,

pray remember that both Goethe's and Boito's Faust, after he had thrown himself into the healthy vortex of life, ended as a practical world-reformer and even redeemed his un-natural contemplative seclusion and asceticism by passion, frailties and *faux-pas* which are not the exclusive monopoly of the unthinking 'practical man of the world.' There are, moreover, purely theoretic and scientific specialists who, with scientific method and in the interest of Truth, without haste—or certainly with less haste than your journalist—deal, not only with problems of physiological life, but with the facts of social life. I am not alluding to the historian and economist, whose preparatory study of the past does not necessarily destroy or weaken his ability to deal with the present and the future; but to the sociologist and publicist. You surely cannot maintain that these students, deeply concerned with the affairs of the life about us, are not capable of ascertaining these facts of life as well as your journalist; that they are not aware of their importance, and that they are not qualified to sift them with regard to their intrinsic values and the bearings which they have upon the needs of the living present and future. It is true that they are not constrained to arrive at their conclusions in one day or one hour; but that, after mature weighing of evidence and much deliberation, they communicate these facts to the world, in a book, a pamphlet, a magazine article, or even in one of our weekly journals, over their signatures. Do you maintain that this greater deliberation removes them further away from the goal of Truth, and makes their opinions less valuable and salutary for the public mind?

Judgment and Haste. "This brings me to the second component in the mental constitution of your ideal journal-ist. It is upon this qualification of his that you have laid greatest stress; the faculty of rapid judgment. I see no need for this. On the contrary, from every point of view, I have been urging the necessity of withstanding the allurements of hasty and premature judgment. In this haste lurks the arch-evil; and the promoters of this evil are the arch-enemies in the intellectual and moral life of the people. You and those who think as you do may answer me by that fallacious shibboleth, which is constantly thrust upon us to account for all superficiality and all frivolous impatience in work and in pleasure—i.e. 'that life is short.' This really seems to imply that there is no time to think and that, though Truth may suffer, we must 'make up our minds,' or what we are pleased to call 'our minds.' Life is no shorter than it was before—nor, let me remind you, is art any shorter. They are both as long now as they ever were. I even believe that our generation (before the war) lived longer than those immediately preceding it. I deny that there is any need of making up our minds rapidly. Speculators on the various Exchanges and those engaged in speculative commercial and industrial enterprises may be obliged, as heretofore, to make up their minds rapidly, almost instantaneously. The difference between former years and now is that the increased means of intercommunication have given our speculators more facts and complicated facts to deal with than the broader outlines of judgment which formed the basis of decision for the speculators and merchants of by-gone days. Such occupations no doubt demand the faculty of rapid decision. But we need not encourage the mental attitude of the speculator and gambler among the general public, and especially not in grave matters of social and political concern. Above all, you and your colleagues, whose duty, after all, it is to establish and to convey truth to the general public, ought not to encourage this mental attitude in them nor even in yourselves. As regards the public, if the facts on which their judgment is to be formed are too complex to enable the mass of the people to have an opinion, the public must then do without opinions on such matters and must withhold them until *responsibly* provided with the material for arriving at a just decision. But you journalists are the last persons—on your own showing—to provide them with this material. For your whole primary attitude of searching for news as such, of cultivating rapidity, or rather haste, in coming to a conclusion, are the very elements which are most opposed to sound judgment. Moreover, consider that you are employed by papers representing the interests of political parties, and, in some cases, definite individual interests of a less exalted and impersonal nature, and that your opinions are bound to be, or at least likely to be, influenced and vitiated by such a bias. Finally, I must ask you, whether your colleague whose paper represents the opposing party-interest, is not likely to form a judgment differing essentially from your own? He transmits his judgment to his paper, you to yours, and both publish them, presenting to a large number of readers views diametrically opposed to one another, which they readily and often passionately adopt as their own. It will then depend upon the circulation of the paper, itself depending upon conditions in no way relating to soundness of judgment and truth, which opinion is accepted by the larger number of people, and thereby ultimately becomes the basis of public policy for the State. What is the final result and where are we as regards the prevalence and endurance of Truth?

Journalistic Form. "In addition to all these dangerous influences, we must consider the third specific characteristic of modern journalism, i.e. the need for striking, emphatic and exaggerated diction, which has developed our journalese style and on which I have dwelt before. This again is bound—or is, at least, likely—to influence your original judgment consciously or unconsciously. As a class, you journalists have every temptation and inducement to be sensational, at times, even hysterical. You are the *last* people in whom I should seek for safe, well-balanced and sober judgment. Many of you, the best of you, will, by a great moral effort, endeavour to suppress and counteract this evil tendency of your profession; and, if not always, you may do it at times. But it is hard to break away from a mental habit.

Summary of Results of Journalism on Truth. "The conclusion at which we are forced to arrive is: that modern journalism acts in a most demoralising manner on the mentality of the modern world. By the essential constitution, as well as the immediate objects and ultimate aims, of the modern newspaper itself, and by the training and professional practice of even the most high-minded journalists, the cause of Truth is far from being furthered; it is in fact injured in its most vital functions and purpose, and Truth, as we have maintained before, is, in its relation to the life of a community and to the world at large, not only a theoretical luxury but a practical necessity upon which the whole well-being of the community depends, even in the most material functions of daily life. Finally, on the negative side, through the encouragement which is given to prepare the mental food for the public in a condensed and highly seasoned form, there has been created a habit and craving for such a condensation and preparation of its mental diet, so that the public mind turns from healthy and simple fare and refuses altogether the nourishment which sustains the truth-providing organs. The world suffers from moral dyspepsia. It is chiefly owing to the journalist, who, as I said before, monopolises most of the leisure which the public devote to reading, that people will no longer read books, which in most cases are the only avenues to sound and beneficent education and to the realisation of Truth. It is also owing to this influence that, when people do read, from the habit of rushing through newspapers, accelerated by the milestones of headlines, they no longer read these books leisurely, carefully and thoroughly, the only method leading to complete, useful and improving understanding. The journalist, more than any other class of men, has helped to lower and vitiate the sense of Truth."

CHAPTER IX.

"RECONSTRUCTION" OF JOURNALISM
BY THE STATE

IF this is the great evil, what practical and effective remedy can be provided to cure it? Though I am fully aware of the discouraging fact that the mere exposition, and even the acceptance, of reforms undeniably desirable in themselves are not enough to counteract the powerfully established traditions that hold our public life in their grip by so many tentacles, I venture to suggest in a constructive spirit the means which may overcome this most powerful danger to the establishment of Truth and its diffusion into public life—in the first place the action which it is possible for the State and public bodies to take, and in the second place, the intrinsic reform of modern journalism as well as the means of publicity in the various forms which the printing press has put at our disposal.

State Inter-ference. We must first consider the desirability and the possibility of the interference of the State and of public bodies to guard Truth in the interest of the public. Here we at once meet with the strong, and in itself, justified, objection against any interference with the Freedom of the Press. The recognition of this great principle in public life is one of the most signal achievements of the nineteenth century, and must be jealously guarded at all costs. It was writ large on the banner of Liberalism through-out all the struggles for freedom in the various enthusiastic movements of the past century. It was often the centre and forefront of the struggles for emancipation from the

trammels of tyranny and feudalism. In spite of the victory
of Liberalism in most parts of the civilised world, some of
the leading countries of Europe are still enslaved by autocracy, and Germany, which took so active and potent a part
in the Liberal Revival and Period of Enlightenment during
the Napoleonic era and in the Revolution of 1848 (and
which in some spheres of intellectual life occupies the first
rank), must emphatically be classed as reactionary in spirit.
As regards the Press, there is no more representative instance of this reactionary spirit than the Press Bureau of
Berlin backed by the *Reptilienfond* from which it draws its
powerful material sustenance. In the interests of Truth, no
more damning instance could be adduced against State-
interference than the working of this Press Bureau. The
natural answer to this objection, of course, is that Germany
has a purely autocratic, or at least, a bureaucratic and
militaristic government, and that the same objections do
not hold in truly democratic countries. We, who happily
enjoy the blessings of a democratic régime, have however
realised from our own experience what such interference
might mean even in the working of the Censorship among
us, an undoubted military necessity during the prosecution
of this war. It has brought home to us, confirmed and in-
tensified, our mistrust of Red Tape and of the unintelligence which seems to go with the security of bureaucratic
authority. The imminence and acuteness of our personal
experiences help to bring home vividly the unintelligence
of the official bureaucratic mind and serve as a warning
against State-interference in matters of moral, intellectual
and artistic interest. Whenever there is a question of thus
invoking the help of the State, there is at once an outcry of
"Save us in all matters of the mind from official intelli-

gence!" This is felt strongly by high-minded and competent educational reformers and by advocates of university reform, and in general by all those concerned in educational matters; though they must not forget that the most drastic and beneficent reforms at the end of the seventies of the last century were carried out with the sanction and under the authority of the State.

Besides this danger, inherent in bureaucratic organisation and in the nature of the bureaucratic mind, we who enjoy the blessings of a democratic government must remember that its freedom is modified by the abuses of party government. Thus the administration of the day is bound, or at least, is likely to influence the working of any such department by the interests or the prejudices and fixed opinions of the party in power. Here again we meet with a grave objection to State influence interfering with the absolute Freedom of the Press. Moreover it may be urged that, through the enactment of copious and elaborate laws against slander and libel, the State has already done its share and has protected the public from offences against Truth in the Press.

Powerful and worthy of attention as all these objections may be, they do not render a thorough and unbiassed consideration of this important problem superfluous. We in no way advocate the establishment of a Press Bureau in degree or in kind similar to that of Germany. Official and semi-official communications can and will be made, the difference only being that they will be more numerous, taking the public more into the confidence of the administration and thereby in turn training the public in its power of apprehending and of judging important matters of State. Nor will the instrument through which the State thus takes direct cognisance of the Press in the public interest (a State, moreover, systematically and directly under the control of the public in its very constitution) be subject to bureaucratic formalism or unintelligence or in any way come within the influence of party government.

What the modern Democracy—which means the modern State—must realise is, first, that Freedom of the Press does not mean Privilege to disseminate Untruth, as little as personal liberty implies freedom to steal or to murder. In the second place, we must remember that the newspaper in its modern position as the principal high road to the knowledge of public events, is in some form a monopoly, on account of this essential attribute of publicity. It is the means of arriving at true information, as much as roads or sign-posts are the means of public transportation and direction, as the postal and telegraphic services are means of public communication. In one sense it is even more *public* in character; for, where letters and telegrams convey private information between individuals, the newspaper transmits public information to the public at large. The State must realise its duty to guard Truth in the interest of the public as it now guards the safety of the roads and communications, the education of the young, as well as life and property.

At present the State cannot directly ensure Truth except through its educational institutions; but it can directly guard the public against untruth. It does this to a certain degree by its laws against slander and libel as regards the individual. But the important point to be realised, is that, so far from granting exceptional privileges to the Press in the freedom of statement and the spreading of reports, it ought still further and more drastically to guard and to protect the individual and the public against the dangers of untruth, in consideration of the fact that the potency and facility of diffusing facts and opinions and of ensuring publicity, inherent in the Press, constitute, as it were, a monopoly of the same nature as are the construction of public roads, and the postal and telegraphic services for purposes of communication. The very granting of such legal privileges to some extent constitutes the establishment of a monopoly. In any case, however, it must be recognised that, harmful as the invention and spreading of untrue statements by an individual within the circle of his own influence may be, the publication of inaccurate or untrue statements through the one vehicle, the direct aim and purpose of which is such publication and the widest diffusion among the whole population, is against "public policy" and must therefore be prevented by the State in protection of its national life.

Now this can be done, first, by the reform of the Press-laws and the modification of "privilege" with regard to libel, and, in the second place, by the establishment of an independent department, judicial as well as administrative, to carry these laws into effect. But we may even go a bold step forward and advocate the assumption of the function of distributing truthful information by the State and, in the future, by the administration of the League of Nations or the International Court backed by Power.

No doubt the laws of libel and slander (which we have discussed above, see pp. 80 seq.) are contrived to protect the individual and the public against defamatory statements. They are designed emphatically to check all words and deeds manifestly arising out of the motive of hatred and malice. No privilege granted to individuals, or newspapers protecting them, against penalty for true or untrue statements made by them holds, if "malice" can be proved. It will, however, readily be perceived how difficult it is to prove "malice" as a motive in a Court of Law. Any defamatory statement which "exposes a person to hatred, ridicule or contempt or which causes him to be shunned or avoided or which has a tendency to injure him in his office, profession or trade is slanderous or libellous." However, unless these conditions are fulfilled, the mere statement of an untruth is not libellous unless "malice" can be proved. Now, I maintain emphatically, that an essential difference ought to be established between the legal meaning of "publication" in newspapers and in less public channels of communication. For in the first place, the designed and deliberate publication of facts defamatory, injurious, or even merely causing annoyance, always implies *malice* in the act. The practice of English law confirms this view in the very difference established between libel and slander; for (as we have seen before) the former is the more serious offence because the written or printed statement is of itself recognised as a graver offence than the spoken word. An individual may inadvertently or in a momentary fit of temper speak or write words thus defamatory; but this does not necessarily prove deliberate malice. On the other hand, deliberately to write, to cause to be set up in type, to correct and then hand over to the machinery of the widest instrument of publication, (as lasting as is the life of paper and print,) apart from any serious injury, and even if it only be disagreeable to the victim, does imply malice—which means the desire to harm. In the second place, unless "special damage" or the other injurious results mentioned above result, a statement is not slanderous or libellous even if it can be proved to be untrue. But as we have seen, an essential difference ought to be established between the legal meaning of "publication" in newspapers and in the other methods of private communication. They are the privileged vehicle of truthful information and partake of the nature of a monopoly. Their function, like that of a railway which controls traffic, is diverted and vitiated when untruths are conveyed, and in that case the privilege ought to be withdrawn. The spreading of lies is a damage to the public. Apart from "special damage" to any individual, there is damage to the public. Even if it be a trivial or "innocent" lie, it becomes a "public nuisance" as unhealthy and disagreeable smells or distressing noises are recognised as such. Misleading the public, even without any "special damage," is, finally, injurious to the moral health of the public, as smells and noises may be detrimental to physical health.

The Press-laws ought therefore to be modified, not only to include direct punishment for the spreading by the newspaper of untrue statements of whatever nature—but also to provide for the adequate and immediate correction of such statements. The newspapers ought to be bound, with the least possible delay, to publish apologies and retractions upon being notified of misstatements. These apologies and retractions ought to be published at once so as to make them as effective as possible, and any delay ought to constitute an aggravation of the offence should further legal proceedings follow. Furthermore, they ought to be made practically in the same form and in the same part of the newspaper where the untrue statement was originally made. The justice of this condition will be manifest. For it is often the practice of newspapers to make the misstatement in a conspicuous form, perhaps on the most important page containing foreign news and telegrams, and to relegate their apology or correction to an inconspicuous column or corner, in the smallest print. Every paper, moreover, might establish, within reasonable possibilities for the adjustment of their limited space, some portion of each issue for corrections of its statements, clear and concise, which are not defamatory, but which will, by the publication of such corrections, further the transmission of Truth and, at all events, guard against the diffusion and confirmation of Untruth.

The insurance of these ends, more important and more urgent in their necessity than many material reforms now admitted by the public and the Government, would no doubt open the doors to a vast amount of business and of work with which our over-loaded Courts of Law could not be expected to deal, even if they were the proper administrators of such law. It would therefore require the establishment of a special Press Arbitration Court, beyond all influence of *party* administration, half administrative and half legal, yet wholly judicial in spirit, in which the interests of the community in the transportation and communication of the most important and vital moral goods should be guarded.

Now I venture to go still further and to suggest far more extensive, direct and active intervention on the part of the State in matters journalistic. This will no doubt meet with much opposition supported by cogent arguments from many points of view. The chief objection will come from those who do not consider matters spiritual, intellectual and moral to be suitable to direct action on the part of the State.

This question supplies us with reasons for my chief impeachment,—not only of reactionary Conservatism, Capitalism and all those who are directly bent merely upon preserving privilege, whether conferred by birth or by money, but also of the Socialist and Labour parties,—that they have all raised the economic factor in private and public life to a

height of all-predominating importance and have not
properly co-ordinated it in the general sociological system,
in which, whatever its importance, it must be subordinated
to wider, as well as more fundamental, moral and social aims
and ideals. No doubt the professional economists and
economic writers for the last hundred years and more are
responsible for this distortion of facts. The misleading
arrogation of social welfare in the implied connotation of
the terms "Socialism" or "socialistic," as covering the whole
of human life and the interests of civilised society, corresponds to the same truth-distorting abuse of the term "international" by the Marxian socialists, with whom it merely
refers to class-antagonism and the final dominance of one
class and one group of human occupations over the rest.
Thus the modern cry for "nationalisation" of transportation, of railways, of mines, of the provision for all the
economic necessities of life—in fact of all industry—has
entirely ignored the most important and natural factor in
national education, namely, the transportation of truthful
information and news. From the nature of things, this is
the department in which "nationalisation" should first be
called for and carried into effect and is, moreover, a department in which it can easily be realised.

There, no doubt, now exists an Official Gazette with us as
in most other countries. But the information conveyed is
generally confined to announcements concerning the mere
machinery of government on the more personal side. In
many countries there exists an official Press and in most
countries statements are conveyed throughout the whole
Press more or less clearly indicated as "official," "semi-
official" or "inspired." But what, in the first instance, is
most urgently called for is that such sources of official information should be clearly and unequivocally stated and

Journalism by the State

Journalism by the State

Journalism by the State   141

impressed upon the reading public and that such information should cover the whole of foreign as well as of domestic politics, enactments and administrative action and policy. No doubt there now exists the useful custom of "questions and answers in the House." But this source of information is fortuitous and—from the nature of party government and procedure—biassed in origin and statement. It ought to become one of the most important official functions and practices of each administration thus to inform, as well as to educate, the general public in matters of State and, above all, to ensure truth and the resultant faith in the public mind.

Such a practice would be far from making a new departure in public life. The Herald and the Town Crier and the "proclamations" posted conspicuously on the Town Hall or the village church were, from the remotest antiquity, the means of making public announcements by the local or central authorities. With the growth and development of political life, of democracy, of the direct participation of the larger population in self-government, as well as the vast increase of public business, of the interrelation and interpenetration of public and private life and interests, the need for public information has grown infinitely greater than it was in the days when the King's Herald or the Town Crier sufficed to keep the people informed of the facts which it was thought needful for them to know by those who ruled them. The accurate imparting of matters of essential concern to a democratic people should not be left to chance, to the personal bias or personal and party interests of those who have chosen the lucrative business of producing newspapers. By all our experience of the past and the immediate present, the further extension, the systematic official development of this most important function of State is urgently called for.

We next come to the important subject of Advertisement, which plays so predominant a part in the history of Journalism and in the whole of modern economic and social life. We need not be very old to remember the comparatively small sheets issued, generally under the local name of "Advertiser," consisting wholly of advertisements without journalistic news or comment. Out of this sheet, in many cases, by organic stages of commercial and journalistic evolution, some of the most important and prominent newspapers have grown. These sheets responded to a real need in the community, namely, the giving of information—generally local—of commercial, and economic as well as social importance to the community. It marked the step from private to public interest—of the same character and to the same degree as the transmission of letters and telegrams among individuals and public bodies—nay, to a greater degree in so far as the communication is professedly and actually made to the public as such. Now I maintain that this function is essentially one implied by, and inherent in, the very nature of democratic government.

If this be so from the very nature of Advertisement and its essential function, it becomes confirmed and still more urgently desirable when we realise its more indirect influence on journalism in commerce and general intercourse as well as its effect upon the moral, and even physical, health of the whole population in modern times. It will be at once admitted, by all conversant with the management and business of the modern newspaper, that the department of advertising plays an important, if not a dominating, part in the actual working—the production as well as the distribution—of the paper. Without advertisements most modern newspapers could not be issued at all in their present form. It is ultimately this one element which gives them their inordinate power, out of all proportion to the moral, intellectual and political claims of those who are responsible for its writing and production. Is it for the public good that this power should be vested in them? Ought it not to be in the hands of the public itself through the representative government which it has chosen? Moreover, as I have suggested before (see p. 108), the direct influence of those who furnish the newspapers with, or who control, the advertisements themselves, may be great and may be used for private purposes far removed from the public interest. Finally, the announcements thus made direct to the public (and, as we have seen, in so far "privileged" and forming a monopoly) may be immoral and unsocial and "against good policy." Though positive indecency and immorality are forbidden by law, it is practically impossible to control all publications which, insidiously and by clever subterfuges, do convey such reprehensible information, nor can the less open suggestions which lead to demoralisation form the subject of a direct prosecution.

On every ground it is therefore desirable and urgent that the State should directly take charge of this department of public information. The "precedent" tradition is admitted, inasmuch as the State already exacts a tax on advertisements. Here will be found a very important and equitable source of public revenue (local central, or both) more lucrative and more justified, on the ground of *direct* publicity, than are Post and Telegraph. But this "nationalisation" of the definite function of advertisement can and ought to be extended beyond the newspaper to all forms of advertisement, i.e. to every kind of public announcements, which have in modern times developed to such a degree that they

have degenerated into public nuisances. The extensive obtrusion on the public of private concerns all over the country
and in every variety of form—the hypertrophy of modern
advertisement—has assumed proportions and definite forms
which, so far from being in the public interest, have become
a serious evil and nuisance. Enough has already been said
and written on disfigurement of scenery and other abuses to
which the advertising practice has given rise, to the evils of
leading the public to use medicines detrimental to health,
besides the more directly immoral or harmful commercial
interests which are thus unduly obtruded and favoured by
public announcements. Whoever has walked through the
streets of many a town, more especially in America, must
have had his nerves shattered, not only by the Babel of
sounds and noises, but by the bewildering forms of illumin-
ated and revolving announcements by means of which the
advertiser literally *forces* even the most reluctant and peaceful citizen to take note of his often useless or fraudulent
incitements to purchase his wares. Police regulations protect us against evil smells and the harmless street-organ can
be prevented from disturbing the repose of a given district.
Surely we have a right to claim protection from sight-
stenches and sound-stenches as well as from noxious gases[1].
The necessary result of this whole system of advertisement,
less direct, though equally opposed to the well-being of the
public, is the increase of neurasthenia among the people of
our own days, because the State does not perform a duty
which lies within its real province and leaves it to the
cupidity of individuals, who, moreover, do not perform the
important function of conveying truthful information to the

[1] I am informed that one Government department specially forbids
in its leases the use of such flashing illuminations for advertisements.

public and of directing it into the channels which benefit instead of injuring public health, both physical and moral.

Let no one object that the establishment of such public departments will encourage bureaucratic tyranny and will not attain the desired ends. Such objections spell the impeachment of democracy and the glorification of autocracy. The democracy can and must control its own officials and remove those who are corrupt or inefficient—or go under[1].

[1] Mr Sydney Brooks, an experienced authority on matters journalistic, has kindly read the manuscript of this book with a view to making suggestions and corrections. He advises me to carry my study of the subject still further and to enter upon the historical consideration of the whole question of Publicity. Such an *exposé* would be out of place here; but an exhaustive monograph on Publicity is urgently called for. In an illuminating letter, following upon a conversation we had after he had read this book, he made these most suggestive comments on the wider question:

"The problem of Journalism in its relation to the State and the individual citizen and international affairs and even life in general is only part of the bigger problem of publicity. No one that I know of has yet attempted to work out the action and reaction of the new and tremendous power of publicity upon the scheme of things. Probably we are still too near to the eruption of this strange force that has burst upon the world to be able to assess its significance or formulate its relations to life and government and society. A generation still lives which saw the birth of Journalism in its present form. It is the product of a quick succession of astonishing inventions. The railroad, the cable, the telegraph, the telephone, the rotary press, the linotype, the manufacture of paper from wood-pulp, these are the discoveries of yesterday that have made possible the journal of to-day.

"But already the Press seems to have taken its place among the permanent social forces. We see it visibly affecting pretty nearly all we do and say and think, competing with the churches, almost superseding Parliaments, elbowing out literature, rivalling the schools and universities, above all furnishing the world with a new set of nerves. What seems to me to mark out our age from all others is precisely this ubiquitous phenomenon of publicity. The ancient world had religion, art, law, commerce, and war. And it also had in the old City-States publicity on an intense but of course very local scale.

International Control. So far from being deterred from urging this thoroughly practical reform in public life and even State intervention, by the inevitable objection on the ground of "practicability" or the condescending and con-

But Journalism, the reading habit, the penetration of the printed word—these are peculiarly modern accessories. The whole world of to-day lives in a glass house with all the electric lights turned on and a reporter at each key-hole and staring through every pane; and it is odd that nobody has yet tried to trace out the consequences of this new and pervasive force, to define its nature and functions, and to establish its place and prerogatives by the side of those other influences that were equally operative in the past as in the present.

"All industrial problems, and the whole spirit in which industry is conducted, are profoundly affected by the fact that nowadays the workers *know*, or at any rate hear of, read about and discuss things that their grandfathers were either altogether ignorant of or accepted uninquiringly as part of the ordained order. Similarly the flounderings of the British Government in its efforts to gauge or influence opinion at home and abroad are due at bottom to a failure to adjust the official mind to this formidable force of publicity."

I have always held that, from the Herald of olden days, the Town Crier and the notices exhibited in public places, publicity concerning affairs and matters of State has passed through three main phases: (1) the public meetings of citizens in such City-States as Athens and republican Rome and the speeches there made by the orators and political leaders; (2) parliamentary debates, when representative government was established in modern times, in which the discussion by the members was meant to convince and to affect the decision of the political representatives of the people. There can be no doubt that this effect was produced in earlier days by actual debate; while, with the development of stereotyped party organisation and government, debate has actually lost most of its effectiveness in directing opinion or voting; (3) the transmission of facts and arguments concerning political affairs through the Press to instruct and influence the electors themselves.

In the first stage, owing to the comparative restrictions of space and numbers of inhabitants, the orator could directly influence the voters with whom the decision rested. This no doubt presented great advantages, though it gave too much power to oratory itself, often led to the victory of the demagogue over the statesman and patriot

temptuous sneer of the worshipper of established formalism, I even venture to go further and to express the hope (already suggested on p. 136) that some day in a future not too remote,

and was, in its emotional effectiveness, likely to arouse popular passion and to lead to hasty decisions.

In the parliamentary period some of the evils resulting from the influence of mere oratory still made themselves felt; but, with the growth of party government, the electors not forming an assembly directly producing or modifying the laws, the machinery for furnishing the means of instructing the voter on both sides of the question has grown perfunctory.

With the imperfections of the Press in this respect I have dealt in the text, especially in so far as it is a party-press. The evils are not so much to be found in what is reported and said as in what is not reported and left unsaid.

The problem and its solution become the more complicated and the more urgent the greater the extent in space and in the numbers and variety of the population in States like the British Empire. The more democratic the country and with the constant enlargement of the franchise, the greater grows the need for the truthful and effective instruction of the voters concerning the facts and arguments with which they have to deal in the interest of the whole people. There can be no doubt that the Referendum, already actually in use in such countries as Switzerland, will ultimately have to be introduced into all democratic countries, when it concerns decisions on definite questions of vital national importance. This, of itself, pre-supposes or pre-demands that the State itself should take charge of publicity as affecting popular decisions.

There have been isolated anticipations, under our present embryonic—or rather chaotic—practice of publicity. So in France, by decree of the State, notable speeches by statesmen on important issues, have by public enactment been printed and posted throughout the country in order to reach as far as possible the whole population. In a lesser degree the occasional publication of discussions by those qualified in the "Letters to *The Times*" (one of the characteristic and undying achievements of that paper) has pointed in the same direction. Difficult as the problem undoubtedly is, the regulation of Publicity by the State is one of the necessary consequences of democratic government and will have to be faced and solved in the near future.

it will be possible to extend the effective insurance of Truth beyond the internal government of each nation into the wider sphere of internationality, and that there will be an International Bureau, organised by the League of Nations, or, as I still venture to hope, by the "International Court backed by Power," in which "foreign" transgressions of Truth in journalistic publication will be dealt with and rectified. That this is not the unpractical and Utopian dream of a visionary, I can prove from having been personally concerned, some twelve years ago, in the establishment of a great international news-agency, which was on the eve of actual realisation, the object and aim of which was the insurance of Truth in the transmission of international news. This important and practical scheme (such it has since been called by one of the most eminent and successful business men of America, controlling the interests of vast telephone and telegraph companies) was designed as a pure business concern, with a capital of £1,000,000, and was supported by practical business men of wealth and prominence in various parts of the world, who realised that the introduction of the moral element which made for truth, constituted the most valuable business asset in the whole scheme. The story of "this enterprise that failed," partly through the more or less accidental mismanagement and partly through certain characteristics in the personality of one man who had the making or undoing of it in his hands, is of such great public interest, that I propose to make it fully known to the world at an early opportunity. While refusing to have any responsibility in, or to be in any way directly concerned with, the financial and business side of this great enterprise, I undertook at the time to be the head of the "moral" side. This "moral" department, to which was ensured final control and direction of the business side, had already succeeded in forming national committees in each of the principal countries of the civilised world, composed of the most eminent and honourable men of every class, who were to act as a court of direction and appeal to ensure Truth in the transmission of all news and articles issued by this international agency. In addition, there was to be established a final Court of Appeal, at The Hague, consisting of delegates from the various national committees meeting there for a definite period in every year, to which appeals from the decisions of the national committees could be referred for final rectification, as also all complaints and differences arising between the business management and the moral committees of control. Had this great scheme been realised in working efficiency for some years before the advent of this war, I do not claim that it could at once have effectually prevented the outburst; but I am justified in believing that the information and education of the public all over the world might have contributed greatly, if not to the relinquishment of the set policy of any one country, at least to the full comprehension of that policy by the peoples of all the other countries. Perhaps, even more than in the home life within each nation—great as is the need there also of preventing the wilful diffusion of untruths—the almost grotesque manufacture of lies through the agency of the Press in every country[1], in order to produce estrangement

[1] A striking illustration is furnished from my own personal experience. In 1897, at the close of the Graeco-Turkish war an article appeared in the *Gegenwart* of Berlin (one of the most trustworthy and respectable weekly papers in Germany) on the origin of that war. It contained a series of signed letters by men eminent in science and learning in that country, evidently founded upon, or inspired by, information received from the German Foreign Office,

and animosity between the several nations in the international world, will have at all costs to be counteracted and the immediate crying necessity of upholding the cause of Truth among the several nations will be felt. This need will be felt so urgently, that the beginnings of the great reform may come from the wider international body at once, and thence penetrate downwards into all the paths and byways of our internal national life.

and showing how, even at that period, popular opinion as directed—or rather wilfully misled—by the German Government was preparing the mentality which has led to the present world catastrophe. The object was to produce or aggravate mistrust and hatred among the German people against England. The contribution of the famous philosopher, the late Eduard v. Hartmann, maintained the absurd contention that England was directly responsible for that war, as it was also for the Armenian massacres, having incited the Greeks as well as the Armenians to take up arms in order perfidiously to further her own political interests. As I happened to be well acquainted with the official attitude of the British Government towards Greece, and possessing irrefutable evidence that every step was taken by England to prevent Greece from taking up arms, I wrote a reply to Eduard v. Hartmann with an urgent request to the editor that, in the interest of truth—if for no other reason—my reply should be published in the *Gegenwart*. In spite of the support of many eminent and influential people in Germany it was impossible to secure publication either in the *Gegenwart* or in any other German paper.

CHAPTER X.

"RECONSTRUCTION" OF JOURNALISM FROM WITHIN

IF the State, through the modification of its laws and through the establishment of an administrative machinery which should control journalistic work, in order to prevent the spread of untruths, may contribute to this "consummation devoutly to be wished," the most important reform will still be the complete revision of journalism from within, in the proper and true adjustment of the journalist's profession and career and the direction of journalistic activity of the newspapers themselves.

We have seen that the influence of the modern journalist, though he has an ideal conception of his training and profession, is unfavourable to the maintenance and refinement of Truth through the development which the modern newspaper has undergone. The newspaper must return to its original purpose and destination of a *news' paper*. In the training of the journalist to fulfil these aims, there remains a wide and important sphere to work upon. The "lightning reckoner," who forms opinions and judgments with lightning speed, must go. There will still be room for thorough and conscientious training, even if we do not admit the actual necessity or utility of definite Schools of Journalism. The management of a newspaper requires, not only inborn talent, but continuous work, the training and experience of a lifetime. It is a profession or trade in itself as complicated as any other one of our great professions. From the mastery of the technique and business of printing to the due disposal

of the space available in each number of the paper, with a
view, not only to its distribution and regulation, but to a
fixed system determined by the division of subjects which
the reader requires to find in their proper places, and, above
all, to the due proportion in the distribution of such information and news in consideration of the intrinsic nature
and importance of each item; in the department of advertisement, the financing of the paper, etc., etc.—the grasp and
mastery of all these several requisites and demands which go
to the production of a successful newspaper will tax the
capacity, the industry, experience and judgment of the ablest
men within a community, quite apart from their prestidigi-
tator tricks of rapid, and in so far misleading, judgments of
the actual affairs of the world of life and thought.

*The News'
Paper.*

If the journalist himself thus returns to his
true and nobly important function, the newspaper itself must become the purveyor of all
important news and information with the greatest rapidity
and accuracy. This, in all conscience, is a task of sufficient
importance and difficulty. It will also become, as heretofore,
the means of distributing official information given by the
State and all its departments, such information growing in
frequency and fulness with the growth of the truly democratic spirit among the citizens of a country, together with
the advancement of their political education and the realisation of their political responsibilities. But the opinions and
judgment of proprietors, editors, foreign correspondents and
leader-writers, given in lightning succession day by day, are
to be expunged from the sheets of the daily press. The
functions of the editorial staff and the leader-writers must
be limited to explanatory comment in order to increase the
intrinsic understanding of the news conveyed—comments of

a geographical, political, economical, statistical and ethnographical nature.

One important result of this curtailment of journalistic activity, the material and practical consequences of which will be far from negligible, will be a great diminution in the bulk of the daily newspaper and of the reading-matter forced upon the public in these days of rapid intercommunication, of which we have heard so much, and the recognition of which has led to such harmful developments of journalism. We may even hope that, with the introduction of some invention in the mechanical printing and folding of paper, the inconvenient folio size of our daily papers may be reduced to more manageable and convenient proportions. I venture to express the opinion—not the result of one day's thought and experience—that a newspaper, which was backed by sufficient talent and capital and boldly set out to limit itself to the publication of really important news without personal comment, presented in the most effective manner, and adopting the more convenient quarto or even octavo form, would prove a great financial success for the experienced newspaper-man who would undertake such an enterprise on a large scale.

As for the formation of opinion and judgment on such news and matters of public concern, on which the wider public requires further instruction and guidance, I have already referred above to the work of the publicist, economist, sociologist and other students as well as men interested in public affairs, who have prepared themselves by training and experience to form such opinions, the expression of which is not only right and useful, but is for them a duty. My contention, and my condemnation of one-sided journalistic activity, are entirely concerned with the

element of rapidity and haste in the formation of judgment
and with the consequent conception which the journalist
has of his career as fitting him for the expression of such
opinion within the shortest time on all matters that concern
the public. The editorial "we" should be abolished. In its
place the expression of opinion and judgment must be
clearly presented to the public over the signature of the
writer, so that the public can gauge the *prima facie* qualifications and authority inherent in the opinion expressed—in
fact the question whether such an authority has the right to
an opinion on such matters at all.

Periodical Literature. For the publication of opinions there remain
the weekly newspapers, including the bulky
weekly editions of the daily papers as developed more especially in the United States, which inci-
dentally convey so much useful general information, the
more useful when it emanates from distinguished authorities
in the various intellectual spheres, whose signatures are af-
fixed to their articles. There further exist the monthly and
quarterly reviews and magazines for this definite purpose.
All these again increase their utility and further the ultimate
objects of Truth the more the articles show the definite
authorities from whom they emanate.

Pamphlets and Books. Finally, however, there remains a most important domain, in the publication of mature
and deliberate thought on matters that vitally
concern public welfare, which cannot be condensed and
cramped into the shorter compass of periodic publication.
It is eminently untrue that whatever is worth saying can be
said in a few words. Aristotle's condensed statement of the
essential principle of all art, as being concerned with the
"harmony between form and matter" (in spite of its own

shortness), conveys one of the deepest truths. Now, some "matter" can "harmonise" with a shorter form of exposition, other subjects essentially require a longer form. The weightier matter requiring the fullest and most thorough treatment demands the book-form. On the other hand, some important information, generally concerned with one definite topic or condition of affairs, is also often not suited to a longer monograph or book. Moreover, the manufacture of a book requires comparatively much time; while the expression of such opinions as I have in view, though in no way calling for haste, still requires for its effectiveness the most rapid publication. There remains therefore one form of publication, widely prevalent in former days, the return of which I wish to advocate—i.e. the signed pamphlet. It must be admitted that this is the best form in which opinions and judgments can be adequately expressed by those qualified to hold them. The great difficulty remains in our days the adequate means of distribution. In exceptional cases, such as some of Mr Gladstone's pamphlets, the burning interest taken by the public in the questions themselves and the exceptional popularity and eminence of the author ensured their widest diffusion. Here again I venture —I hope not presumptuously—to make a suggestion of the practical nature of which I have no doubt. If a thoroughly qualified firm of publishers would make it recognisedly its main business to publish such pamphlets, perhaps even adding all the lucrative accessories of the advertising business (hateful and inconvenient as many of us find them, because they inflate the books and magazines), I have little doubt of ultimate success on the business side, as I have still less doubt that the revival of such a tradition would act most beneficially in diffusing among the public various opinions and judgments on public matters which will ultimately establish Truth, instead of the misleading and demoralising vehicle of our own days—the anonymous daily paper.

Atrophy of Thorough Reading.
Finally I must recur to another point, to which I have referred on several occasions before, i.e. the atrophy of the faculty of sustained and thorough reading of books. Besides all the dangers and evils arising out of the monopoly of modern journalism, upon which we have been dwelling, including the absorption of leisure for reading among the wider public, one of the most disastrous and lasting ultimate effects is, that the public has been turned from the reading of books, and hence from the acquisition of accurate information and the formation of the habit of systematic thinking, which culminate in the love and passion for Truth. It is, after all, this pernicious preaching of the Doctrine of Haste and the daily repercussion of its principles in the hasty, inaccurate or untrue presentation of grave and weighty opinion in the newspapers, which has led to this demoralisation in the mentality of the modern public. Worse than all, with it has come the loss of the habit, and even the distaste for, the thorough reading of longer publications, such as books. It is against this central disease of modern mentality, this cancer eating into the healthy fibre of intellectuality, that I am solemnly and fervently urging all right-minded people to wage war. Truth on matters of importance *cannot* be acquired in haste. The market-place of action may present the *material* for thought; but it is not the place for thought. The silent study will ever remain the workshop where the hard metal of fact—the gold that may be fashioned into a ring—is wrought into lasting and beneficent form. The silent study will always remain the sanctuary of Truth, and it is for us to keep it undefiled.

PART III.

RELIGIOUS TRUTH

In my book *Aristodemocracy* (Part III. Chap. VII.) under the heading "Duty to God," I have endeavoured to define in outline man's duty to Truth in relation to his highest ideals. I must refer the reader to that chapter. But I may here quote one passage (pp. 347-348):

In man's ethical progression through human functions as such, through the objects which man wishes to produce or to modify in nature, he is necessarily led to his ultimate duties towards the world as a whole, not only the world as his sense and perceptions cause him to realise it, *as it is*, with all the limitations which his senses and his powers impose upon him; but the world as his best thought, and his imagination, guided by his highest reason, lead him to feel that *it ought to be*—his ideal world. This brings him to his duty towards his highest and most impersonal ideals of an ordered universe, a cosmos, and of unlimited powers beyond the limitations of his capacities —his duty to God. Ethics here naturally, logically, necessarily, lead to and culminate in, religion.

The supreme duty in this final phase of ethics, man's religious duties, is truth to his religious ideals. It is here, more than in any other phase of his activities, that there can and ought to be no compromise. This is where he approaches the ideal world in all its purity, free from all limitations and modifications by the imperfections of things temporal and material, as well as his own erring senses and perceptive faculties. There are no practical or social relationships, no material ends to be considered, no material interests to be served or advantages gained. The only relationship is that between himself and his spiritual powers and the highest ideals which these enable him to formulate or feel. His duty, therefore, is to strive after his highest ideals of harmony, power, truth, justice and charity. Nor does this function of the human mind and this craving of the human heart require exceptional intellectual power or training. On the contrary, the history of the human race has shown that at every phase of human existence, even the earliest and most rudimentary, in the very remote haze of prehistoric times, the presence of this religious instinct and man's effort to satisfy it are manifested, even though it necessarily be in the crudest, the most unintelligent and even barbarous forms of what we call superstition and idolatry.

Thus in all other spheres of life, man cannot claim absolute certainty. The exigencies imposed upon us by the outer world, in order to realise our convictions in action, make compromise and adaptation to these outer conditions necessary. In most cases we cannot there expect or claim *absolute* certainty; we can only deal with probability and preference. Though we cannot always be sure that the line of action we have chosen is the absolutely correct, the only right one, we need have no doubt of the justification of our opinions and actions if we are satisfied that the balance of evidence, the highest probability, and therefore, our justified preference, lie in this one direction. There need be no doubt at least as regards the certainty of such preference; and our action need in no way be impeded or weakened in its energy, because we cannot attain the absolute.

There is only one sphere in which there is no room for compromise, i.e. our inner self and our relation to our highest ideals. They must in absolute truth be our highest ideals, and no lowering of them is admissible without destroying the life and soul of them. Any compromise, any admission of dogmas and beliefs which we do not hold to be true, are, in the noblest and deepest significance of these symbolic words, a Sin against the Holy Ghost.

But these deepest and noblest thoughts and feelings are in danger of being blunted and coarsened by frivolous and continuous expression and repetition. It is a right instinct, for instance, which keeps us from communicating and publishing broadcast our deepest and most delicate feelings when we are in love. What deeply and truly concerns the inner relation of man to his highest self, his highest ideals, need not be shouted from the housetops.

On the other hand, we are bound in truth to repudiate clearly and unequivocally the misleading adherence to recognised bodies professing beliefs which we do not share, even partially. We cannot subscribe or adhere to a church, creed or sect in the essential tenets of which we do not wholly believe, without committing a sin against the Holy Ghost. Now, I venture to maintain, that if all people were to live up to this sacred duty, we should be astonished to find how large a number of the professed adherents to established creeds and churches are not in truth members of such congregations, and that these dissentients may constitute the best and most thoughtful element now within them. They continue, as far as their profession to the outer world is concerned, to be members of such churches, while in truth they are not. Whatever apparently cogent reasons they may adduce to others or to themselves, they are by their conformity living a lie. If this statement be true, all the established churches are faced with a great crisis in the immediate future—they must choose between reform or revolution.

The Future of the Church. To begin with the great Christian churches—among them the Church of England. It certainly has manifested a tradition in the past admitting of the greatest variety of religious opinion and

shadings of belief within its body, commonly subdivided
into the three familiar groups of "High, Low and Broad";
and within these groups again there were and are varieties
and shadings of definite belief. Now this principle of uni-
versality and tolerance will have to be extended to a far
greater degree if the Church is to survive as the centre of
national belief and as the upholder of the highest Truth.
The real essence of Christianity, as in its purity it stands
before history, will have to be found and confirmed, and
this essence—the moral, spiritual and truly religious essence
—will have to be made the distinctive and all-comprising
condition of its existence: *not wherein people differ but wherein
they agree* lies the essence of all corporate existence justified
in the material and spiritual world. Now, Christianity
stands before the world as the Religion of Love. Christ
stands before the world as the symbol of this Love. The
sayings attributed to Him in the Sermon on the Mount and
other passages in the Gospel, which bear out this all-comprising belief, form the religious essence and spirit to which
all good men and women can and will subscribe. They may
differ on all other points of dogma; but they will and must
agree on this bed-rock of human, social and civilised existence in its truest and highest form. Whatever the theo-
logian, the philologist, the critical historian or the sectarian
controversialist may say, the term Christian as established
in the English language and as used in such phrases as
"Christian love," "the Christian spirit," "the Christian
life," "Christian charity," "the Christian gentleman,"
"Christian civilisation" and "the Christian World" does
connote this meaning. However much in the pages of
history, recording the bloody strife on the battlefield of
militant sectarianism, the burning stake and the torture

chamber, the various churches, sects and creeds may by their acts have belied this essential spirit of Christ-like love, it nevertheless remains stamped on the understanding of modern man as the central meaning in the very soul of his inner religious aspirations. If thus Christ's life and example, ending in the sacrifice of this very life to the highest ideals of religious faith, is made the central, essential and all-embracing doctrine, all shadings of religious belief can be comprised within it, and a Christian Church can gather within its flock all good men and women. There will be no room for sectarian "nonconformity," and the central spirit of Christian Love can and must, in the truth and rightness of its own spirit, be extended to the toleration of all other shadings of belief and doctrine and church government which do not conflict with this central spirit. There will be no need for physical and local isolation of the several groups of Christian religious doctrine and opinion. It will be, and ought to be, physically possible to divide and to distribute the occupation of the existing churches, (which reflect the past historical life of the British nation,) among the adherents of clearly-defined individual differences and shadings of doctrine and belief within the various sects. Different hours for services might be assigned to each sect, while at some times and on some occasions they might all unite in worship in one great national belief. But it must at once be conceded that preference should be given to the Church of England as at present constituted.

The Church of Rome. We meet with the greatest difficulty when we approach the Catholic Church of Rome. But the true and deep meaning of its catholicity ought to give direction and countenance to the realisation of this essentially Christian spirit, beyond the Church of

England, to the whole Christian world. This certainly was
the leading belief and hope in the days of Erasmus and the
educational reformers of mankind, and gave inspiration to
one of the truest and noblest figures in history—Sir Thomas
More. It may be—I fondly believe it is—the beacon-light
of many of those modernists still comprised within the papal
flock, or those who have been forced out of it. After, in the
first place, casting off all temporal claims and aspirations,
it remains for this great historic body to fulfil its destiny in
this world of ours; but it must now face reform, revolution
or ultimate dissolution.

Hebraism and the Jews. We must next examine the difficult problem
concerning the Jewish communities who have
retained the solidarity of their faith in the
western civilised world. In actual life they participate in
what, according to the admitted meaning of the word in the
English language, must be called Christian civilisation.
More than that, they have, in proportion to their numbers,
contributed most effectually to its establishment and advancement in the western world. Whether in their own early
sacred writings, in the precepts of men like Hillel or the later
Rabbinic laws and teachings, they themselves have or have
not in the past established and confirmed, independently
of the Christian churches, Christ's religion of Love, they can
and must subscribe to it in all that is essential. The great
historic truth remains, that Christ in His earthly life was a
Hebrew, and there was thus full justification for the division
which Matthew Arnold made of the two main currents of
modern civilisation into Hebraism and Hellenism. It might
thus with some justice be urged by the Jews that the name
for this universal church of the future should be, not the
Christian, but the Hebraic Church. This contention would

receive additional support from the fact that Christ Himself, in all His direct statements bearing upon the question of nationality and church, considered Himself a Jew—and moreover the true Jew and the upholder of the true Jewish Church. The early Christian Church for many years, perhaps centuries, held the same view; and the Romans considered the early Christians Jews and designated them as such. Even in the fifteenth chapter of the Acts of the Apostles we have evidence of the first traces of antagonism between the Judaic and the Universalistic conception of the Christian faith; the thirteenth chapter still shows the tenacity with which adherence to the Judaic ritual and the preferential position of the Jewish race dominated the original Christian faith and Church.

But, whatever may thus be urged, and rightly urged, in favour of the predominant share of Judaism in the origin and development of the Christian faith, and even of the Christian Church, the fact remains, that the Pauline conception of a catholic, a purely and widely human and universal faith and church, prevailed. On the other hand the Jewish faith and the Jewish Church have always been marked, as an essential feature of that religion, by—at least—some preferential position assigned to the Jewish people and race, and this has been strengthened—with effective practical results in history—by some of its rites. Whatever be the supreme sentimental, historic and poetic justification of Zionist aspirations, recent political developments—which must, moreover, strike a resonant and sympathetic chord in the hearts of all people possessed of imagination and faith in the justice of human history—have clearly shown, that the Jewish faith and Jewish ideals include national ideals, even the most nefarious and misguided form of these—namely, ethnological nationalism. Moreover, in spite of the just and true efforts of such truth-loving and high-minded writers as Matthew Arnold, the terms Hebrew and Hebraic do not and cannot connote in English and most modern European languages the meaning which the term "Christian," as we have defined it, conveys.

If this be true and if those of Jewish racial origin or the adherents of the various forms of Jewish churches (for they differ among each other almost as much as do the Christian churches) admit the truth of it, the objection to this clearly-established word in the English language ought not to prevent their adhesion to such a truly Catholic church, embodying their own essential ideals as well as those of all other civilised people in the western world[1]. If they look into their own hearts and courageously seek for the true causes of the opposition they may feel towards such adherence, they will find that it is the ever-present survival in their consciousness of the bitterness and antagonism bred of the centuries of persecution which their race and their faith have experienced at the hands of their "Christian" persecutors during successive ages. The curse of these unchristian feelings felt by Jews, justified though they be by past history and present persecutions or prejudice among "Christians," is to be found in the survival of resentment and hatred springing from injustice, even though committed

[1] Some evidence that this is practically possible—nay, that in a definite form it has already been achieved—is furnished by the fact that the various undertakings and institutions carried into such fruitful and effective realization by the Young Men's Christian Association during this war, have had the support and even the active adhesion of professedly Jewish bodies and individuals, in spite of—nay, because of—the designation "Christian" in its true and noble significance.

centuries ago. In the same way, the true stumblingblock to the real political union of the Irish with the English people, though they speak the same language, live under the same laws and have the same ultimate political aspirations, is the potent factor of remote reminiscences in the racial feuds of the Ireland of centuries ago and the injustice shown them in the past by England. The stereotyped antagonism between Jew and Christian corresponds to the antagonism between Jew and Gentile in Biblical times. Now, as the Western Jews use the same language, have contributed to and live under the same laws and customs—in short, the civilisation of the Christian world—and as these "Gentiles" actually form the bulk of the Christian people of to-day, so the artificial sub-division between Jew and Christian ought never to be encouraged by the Jews—in fact, it becomes their duty to remove it entirely from modern life. There exists therefore no reason—the racial isolation having no justification whatever—why those who profess the oldest historic creed of monotheism should not be incorporated in this Catholic Christian Church, with the *essential* creed of which they agree, and worship according to their own special rites in the national churches.

We might even extend this all-embracing power and destiny of such a true church of the future to those who have drawn their inspiration from the Koran. Provided their ultimate ideals are truly the same as those dominating the western world, there is no reason why their own variety of belief should not be embraced within this wide and universal grasp of spiritual truth in the Religion of Love. Then, in the dim future it may at last be possible for East and West to meet.

Man's spiritual life, which rules or ought to rule the body, is guided by the heart and the mind. As regards the heart, St Paul's words "but the greatest of these is Charity" ought to rule. As regards the mind, "the greatest of these is Truth" must be our guide. Both are harmonised by the imagination of man which gives Proportion and Beauty to man's feelings, thoughts and acts and to the things of nature, and leads upwards to the ultimate ideals of man's life and of the universe in God. Whether such a unification of Creeds can or will be realised or not, the one supreme duty for all truthful people remains: not to adhere to any religious sect in any dogmas of which they do not believe, or at least, to make known their disagreement and thus to uphold Truth as the foundation of all morality.

Reprinted from *The North American Review* of Sept. 15, 1903.

APPENDIX I.

THE IDEAL OF A UNIVERSITY

A University is educational because it is scientific; a school
is scientific because it is educational.

It is not so much a question of science taking cognizance of
life, as of life taking cognizance of science.

THERE has never been a period when, as at the present moment,
the question of education—especially of higher university education—has been so prominently in the minds of the English-
speaking nations as a question of practical interest. There are
several causes which have conduced to this widespread and
active interest; though none of these alone can be said to be the
really efficient one. First, a need for reform has been realized
and urged from within, i.e. by the teachers and officials of
universities themselves. Then, public munificence has in England as well as in America been directed towards the universities, and the question has naturally arisen as to the best uses
to which wealth thus bestowed can be put. Lastly, the needs
of actual, material life, the necessity of regulating commerce and
industry—all the arts of peace and war—by the highest intelligence available in the nation, have been felt more strongly than
ever before. It has been realized that those countries are advancing rapidly in which the highest intellectual education is
most directly and immediately brought to bear upon the problems of actual life, and where science and life, so far from
being divorced, are most closely wedded together in united
action towards the increase of public efficiency and prosperity;
while those where this is not the case are likely to fall
into retrogression, whatever may be their natural resources and
the strength of their tradition of national wealth or predominance.

As regards the movement for university reform from within, there have been in America and Great Britain a number of thoughtful and experienced university teachers who have the interests of their own universities at heart, as they constantly bring enthusiasm and intelligence to bear upon the problem of advancing science and improving the intellectual life of the nation to which they belong. Their number in English-speaking countries is great, and they may fairly be said to represent the leaders of the nation's intelligence. In America, I would single out one name among a host, as the man who has done more than any other in following up his expressed views by the actual organization of a university embodying, for the time being, the elements of modern needs in a tangible example and model university, the very establishment of which has gone far to influence the spirit and the work of all the other American universities—I mean Dr Gilman, the first President of the Johns Hopkins University.

In England, the most momentous reform of the great English universities, during more than six centuries of continuous activity, was initiated with the new statutes which came into operation in 1880. This reform, approaching near to a revolution of the whole system, had its origin within the universities themselves, and was supported by the majority of university teachers at Oxford and Cambridge, who (with all fairness to the more conservative students who acted in all conscientiousness) may be said to have represented the most prominent teachers and researchers in the universities and in the country. If, for the sake of symmetry, I were to select one name as a leading representative of this movement, I should single out that of the late Professor Henry Sidgwick of Cambridge.

But the intellectual atmosphere within the universities of both countries had, for a long time, been modified and prepared by the fact that a large number of university teachers in both countries had travelled and studied abroad, especially at the universities of Germany. While there imbibing the current methods of learning and research, they realized the ideals which underlie and actuate the intellectual life of German universities, as well as the elements in which these differed from the ideals

current in their own country. Such comparative study, besides
freeing their minds from provincial prejudice, and raising their
standards of academic efficiency, brought home to them with
great force the crying need for academic reforms in their own
universities.

As regards the action of public munificence: A number of new
universities and colleges have been founded in the United
States, as well as in the provinces of England, by private
generosity. Many of these new American universities are excellent and promising foundations. In many cases, however,
the means supplied are ludicrously inadequate for the maintenance—not to speak of the higher development—of real universities. Frequently these new institutions were started in
localities where there already existed one or more colleges of
ancient standing, which were merely in want of financial support
to rise to a higher state ot efficiency. In a country which has the
inestimable advantage of a large number of higher institutions
of learning, diffused all over the land, the question is not so
much one of extension as of concentration. The injudicious
foundation of such ill-equipped new bodies has not only bur-
dened the land with an intellectual incubus and obligation; but
has seriously jeopardized the development of the older institutions—both together tending to prevent any approach to an
ideal university education and a consequent advance of the
intellectual vitality of the nation. Had the misguided philan-
thropists bestowed their funds for the endowment of new
studies or new chairs in the existing institutions; or better, for
the adequate remuneration of the professoriate; or, better still,
had they transferred their funds unconditionally into the hands
of competent and trustworthy officials to bestow them where
needed—nothing but good could have resulted.

In England, on the other hand, there has been for centuries
a practical monopoly of university education on the part of
Oxford and Cambridge, retarding even the advance of a great
metropolitan university in London. The need for decentraliza-
tion in this sphere of national life has rightly been felt to be
paramount. In recent years, the timely advent of private
generosity has resulted in the foundation of several colleges

and universities in the "provinces," especially in the great manufacturing centres, which certainly tend to supply a crying want, and which may, if wisely directed, lead to the quickening of university life, and to a new era of higher education in the British Empire. But up to the present there is danger lest these foundations, with their short-sighted, hand-to-mouth policies and ideals, may retard and vitiate, rather than advance and elevate, the higher learning of Great Britain. The founder or founders of such bodies insist upon carrying out their own preconceived notions as to the needs, the purpose or the utility of a university, crude notions based upon some individual experience or taste in their own life or education—or even trade. A bias may thus be given to the organization, to the aims and to the spirit of the work, which is far from harmless, which cannot be remedied subsequently when bitter experience has led to the recognition of a mistake; for a bias in the very foundations affects the durability as well as the usefulness and beauty of a structure. There is in the minds of such people either a total absence of ideals, or a mistaken ideal as to the nature and purpose of universities; and their views are rapidly being absorbed by the whole nation, perhaps thus retarding the intellectual advance of an empire.

The thoughtful among us must often realize that "public munificence" is not an unmixed blessing. It is one of the charges which the opponents of congested capital may urge against the possession of great wealth by one person, that the power it gives to an individual may be directed into channels affecting public life and widespread interests *without responsibility*. In fact, any inquiry as to capability, motive or responsibility, where actions decidedly have the character of charity and philanthropy, readily assumes the appearance of the ungenerous and ungrateful. Still, it may fairly be questioned, whether the action of individuals—whose good intentions are unassailable—in giving a positive and definite direction to the spirit and methods of public work, and in affecting the distant future of higher national life by some preconceived theory or conviction held by one to whom the nation would never have looked for guidance in such matters, may not be nefarious.

If the possible evils arising out of misdirected munificence apply to the foundation of universities, they apply to the endowment of scholarships, purses and all other forms of endowment leading or coaxing or bribing the young to learn. These present the readiest, most common and most manifest form of doing something for learning and for the poor, while at the same time it requires least thought and trouble to the donor who wishes "to do the right thing." In former ages, when, on the one hand, national institutions of learning were not organized or readily accessible, or when the learned class of "clerks" was chiefly enlisted from the poor, there was a call for the wide application of such benefaction. But to-day, whatever good may be manifest in individual cases, the need no longer exists —nay, I strongly hold that the existing profusion of such scholarships in schools and universities in England effectively blocks the way to the spread of the highest spirit of education, and that the tendency of further endowments of this kind is to *pauperize the national intelligence*. I do not mean research-scholarships, but those given to support the student at school or university during the period of his preparatory education. The sums recently lavished towards helping the learners would have been more effectively used if devoted to the refinement and elevation of the centres where the highest learning is to be given. I am reconciled to the splendid bequest of Mr Cecil Rhodes, because it embodies, impresses and perpetuates a great idea of significance to the world's history: the international, the uniting power which the higher intellectual life possesses among the nations who represent civilization. The huge sums thus given by Mr Rhodes will not be wasted if they merely serve to bring before the eyes of the world this common tie of humanity and perpetuate this lesson. But the same cannot be said, for instance, of the signal generosity which Mr Carnegie has shown to his native Scottish land. One of the several reasons why England lags behind Scotland in the diffusion of university education among its population lies in the overgrowth of such endowments in England. The present system of scholarships has gone far to jeopardize the traditions of higher learning in England; while in Scotland the appreciation of—nay, the enthusiasm for—learning is one of the most valuable national assets; and I sincerely trust that Mr Carnegie's well-meant philanthropy may not seriously threaten the existence of this national virtue.

Lastly, we come to the strong desire for reform of the university system which is wide-spread among the general public both in England and in the United States.

Both countries have exceptional advantages for the advance of national prosperity in the possession of great capital and of natural resources. But, while Great Britain sees its long-standing position of commercial and industrial predominance threatened, the United States recognizes the stupendous potentiality of its future economic development and is anxious now to prepare for its realization; nay, seeing still farther and deeper, it has misgivings with regard to the period when the fortune inherent in virgin soil and the vigorous, untrammelled spirit of young enterprise will no longer be its peculiar advantage over the competing nations of the Old World.

More and more, though in a vague and loose way, the public has come to realize, on the one hand, the practical use of Science, and, on the other, a deficiency in our educational system which does not produce a sufficiently immediate application of scientific achievement to the needs of actual life. This has been impressed still more forcibly when the competition of a country like Germany in commerce and manufacture is keenly felt, a country, moreover, which is not blessed with any of those advantages in capital or natural resources, or any previous position of vantage from which to begin its onward movement of economic ascendancy. In every class it is being realized that something must be wrong when England appears to be falling back where Germany is advancing. Cheapness of labour alone cannot account for this, especially in view of the advance of American industry and the dearness of labour there. But the merchant and manufacturer find that the principle of organization and direction of work in their own spheres, that the "staff" from the highest to the lowest, are more efficient even when Germans leave home and come into competition in other countries: that the clerks, the travellers, the chemists, the electricians employed from Germany are more efficient and successful. There may be, perhaps justly, some reasons for accounting for this superiority less wounding to our national self-esteem. But it seems to be universally felt by the leaders of our commerce and industries that men are better trained for these practical economic purposes in Germany than they are at home. "Something must be wrong at home," they feel and freely say. "What are our schools and universities for? They must take immediate cognizance of our national wants. They have been going on for years and centuries in their happy-go-lucky old-fashioned way of training clergymen and gentlemen. Let them now respond to the crying needs of life."

The first phase of the movement following upon the indefinite discontent is the one we have now attained to, both in England and the United States. I should like to call this the Technical Phase. And, though I believe in technical education when rightly conceived and rightly pursued, the present is, I sincerely hope, merely a phase of transition in the establishment of the true ideals of national education. Each member of the community made discontented with our educational system through the sensitive channels of material self-interest, desires to see reform or improvement in the immediate sphere of his own narrow horizon. Though not as grotesquely unintelligent as the butcher whose letter a headmaster of a prominent school in one of our great manufacturing towns showed me, their views are the same in kind. The butcher wrote that "he desired his boy to be a good butcher, and that only those subjects should be taught to his lad which would make him that." But the would-be educational reformer who is a merchant demands that our universities, if they are to be of use to the country and have his support, should at once establish Commercial Departments or Colleges. If the industry be concerned with one aspect of chemistry or brewing, or tanning, or weaving, the narrow and disjointed part of "applied" chemistry, the art (or science) of brewing, tanning and textile studies, and every conceivable division of craft and learning are to have their departments, or, at least, are to be directly considered in the teaching of a university. The same applies to agriculture and the other occupations of modern life. That is what, in the minds of such people, is meant by "the universities taking cognizance of life."

In a less grotesque form, eminent men of light and leading have given public expression to views which, if they do not advocate such absurd developments of our national educational system, tend to encourage such views. We are constantly reminded of the great use which universities and men of higher science in Germany are to the advance of national prosperity; but the fact is ignored that in Germany the government and the people at large are by tradition and training prepared to appreciate the utility of such higher education and of higher science, and make direct appeal to the sources of highest information. The German manufacturer is sufficiently well educated to follow sympathetically the efforts of men of pure science, whether in chemistry, in physics, in mathematics, in history or languages and literature, to respect their high vocation and to encourage them in their pursuits. Such a man will, for instance, employ twenty chemists who are carrying on researches in directions remote from the industrial chemistry applying to his immediate manufacture, where in England there are but two chemists carrying on "hand-to-mouth" science for the unimproved production of staple articles which will soon be superseded by new articles evolved out of higher scientific research.

In these views of our advocates of university reform the cart is put before the horse. The applicability of science to the actual needs of economic life is increased and made facile by the intelligent readiness of the public to receive it and, above all, to possess some correct notion of its nature, its province, its methods and aims. The premature intrusion of the "technical" point of view will only retard this reasonable application, as it will lower or stultify the efforts of true men of science.

Even Germany seems for the moment to be contaminated by this lowering atmosphere of technical science which penetrates into all strata of national education. It is not likely to do them much harm, because the traditions and living effectiveness of their highest scientific institutions are so strong that they are bound to predominate, to modify, and to direct the work and the teaching of their technical institutions (nearly all the

The Ideal of a University

teachers of these are drawn from the professoriate of their universities), and the strength of these traditions will probably outlast the momentary contamination before it has reached the core of the intellectual life of the nation. Germany is, in every phase of its intellectual life, at this moment living on the work of its great thinkers and workers of the generations immediately preceding our own, of which Virchow may be the last representative—though a large number of younger university professors are prepared to maintain the spirit of the past in its highest and purest form.

What the German universities have done for their national life, and what they stand for in the eyes of the world, is the establishment and the diffusion of the Spirit of Thoroughness which goes down to the root of things and aspires to the summit of human knowledge. Germany is great in this respect, because the intellectual life of the nation and the educational system have, in their very constitution and in the actual history of their development, been regulated by the highest aims, the highest attainments of intellectual life, in their universities, to which all the lower forms lead or tend. These highest attainments and ideals are not left to themselves as the haphazard result of the lower necessities of education; the schools do not so much produce the universities as the universities infuse their spirit of thoroughness and their intellectual ideals into the schools. Both thus react upon the people and upon the actual material and economic life of the whole nation. The teaching of the industrial sciences, of agriculture, of medicine, nay, of school-mastering, is carried on by men trained in the universities in the spirit of pure science as there cultivated. Thus, as an ever-present force beyond the confines of the universities themselves, in all strata of national life, whether consciously held or indirectly and vaguely felt as a remote tradition, there is before the nation the true ideal of a university.

The possession of true ideals may be one of the most practical, not to say material, assets of an individual or a nation. As it may be the most practical method of setting out on a journey before all things to know exactly the journey's goal, so it is most important in the organization of national education to be clear as to the highest goal in the development of intellectual life. As we often find it important to correct the morbid tendency of the unpractical man, the doctrinaire, the visionary, by reminding him of the impracticability of his ideas and by directing his attention to the physical conditions which decide their realizability—the ways and means—so it may often be necessary to remind the "practical man," the man of action or the opportunist, to look to his fundamental principles and his ideals, and only then to set his practical energies in the direction prescribed by them. This is especially the case when the work is concerned with wider, more general, as well as more fundamental subjects and organizations, which are not ephemeral but which determine the life of a nation for ages to come.

A university is for a nation the nearest approach, as a recognizable, tangible, and living institution, to the ideal of man's intellectual development—as, in another way, the churches are the tangible and recognizable centres of the moral and religious life, and the art academies, museums, and theatres of the aesthetic life, of a nation.

It is not the outcome of vague theorizing, but the result of sober observation and experience, which leads us to conclude that the German educational system is thus efficient because, not only does its whole organization culminate in this highest type, the university, with its pure ideals of science and learning, but because the keynote of the whole intellectual education, down to the elementary schools (*a fortiori* for the technical schools) is struck by this highest form, at once most general and comprehensive as well as special and thorough. It thus penetrates through all layers of society and has become a national characteristic. Life takes cognizance of science. The more civilization advances, the greater becomes the need for the regulation of practice by theory, the more important for each State that universities should be thus efficient and should be organized in view of the highest and purest ideals of science and learning.

This view of a university, however, is far from being the predominant one in England and the United States. The mistake with us is that, until quite recently, the only conception of a university has been purely educational, if not pedagogic. It was considered an establishment for the higher training of a small percentage of the inhabitants in each country, chiefly of the upper or professional classes. It was simply a higher school, really a high school for older boys.

I think it is so important that this fatal misconception should be exposed and that the right view should prevail, that I do not shrink from applying the two methods which the late Bishop Creighton considered powerful instruments of education—exaggeration and paradox. A university, then, differs from a school in that it is not primarily educational; a great part of its function in national life would remain if there were not a single pupil or student within its walls to teach. The spirit of the place should be as different from that pervading a school as—though in quite a different way—the atmosphere of the real practical life which follows upon the university studies is to the graduate entering upon his active vocation in the struggle for existence. Each will produce the greatest effect educationally, the more each is true to its own peculiar spirit. For the moment I choose to ignore the directly educational function of a university; though, by maintaining its impersonal and purest ideal as the national embodiment of highest science and learning, it becomes most efficient as an educational institution for the production of the active and successful as well as cultured citizens.

But the real danger at this moment comes, not so much from the confusion of a university with a school, as from its contamination by the technical spirit. Here lies the real danger. The startling and epoch-making discoveries made of recent years by the application of science to the needs of commerce and industry have at last impressed the unthinking with the use of science, until such tangible use has become the test for its right of existence, the justification for its pursuit. The institutions where "science" is cultivated and advanced are supposed to derive their claim to existence and support from such use, and their organization and work are to be regulated in view of the direct application of science and learning to the needs of life.

Not only in such a view is a narrow and grossly material

aspect of economic life substituted for the whole of the intellectual life of a civilized community; but science is narrowed down to the most irrational conception of applied science, the very nature and function of which are grossly misunderstood. For one instance of applied science which has produced results appreciable by the commercial mind, innumerable attempts and experiments are made in every direction without such results; there is a continuous and vast expenditure of reasoning power about us constantly at work, which never comes to the cognizance of the public and can never be apprehended by the commercial mind. Just as, to use a trite simile, the stupendous fortunes made by one great speculation, which obtrude themselves upon the public notice, are not true tests of the effort and the energy expended in the whole world of finance and commerce, of which nothing rises to the plane of manifest and startling public recognition.

A puerile attempt to organize the study of "hand-to-mouth" science with a view to achieving such signal success in its immediate application, will end in failure. For the weakness of the "technical" aspect of science is, that, not going sufficiently deep, it does not carry science farther. Empiricism in science is most "unpractical," because it leaves to chance what the human mind in its highest theoretical function tends to control. Most of the discoveries and inventions which have had such momentous bearings upon our material and industrial life could never have been made but for the work of the highest scientific theorists, carried on in a spirit in no way technical, which is, in one aspect, opposed to practical application—at all events, ignores it while the inquiry is progressing. I mean scientific work which has no manifest practical application. Examples are innumerable and are familiar to those who are at all conversant with true science. Let me but single out a few.

The most recent invention is perhaps the most startling and, in some ways, the most momentous as regards its effect upon life in our age—I mean Wireless Telegraphy.

Yet I am not overstating my case when I say that this invention is inconceivable without a continuous series of purely theoretical inquiries preceding it. In one sense, it is but a corollary of the general scientific and purely theoretical work, in its bearings upon electricity, done by Faraday, by Sir Humphry Davy in his separation of Sodium and Potassium, and finally by Hertz and Clerk-Maxwell in their theoretical work upon certain electric waves. Perhaps it may be said that the development of most of Modern Physics, in its minutest practical applications, could not have been achieved without the purely theoretical work of Sir Isaac Newton grouping round his discovery of the law of gravitation.

The work of Pasteur, whose whole life illustrates the realization of the highest scientific ideals, has led to the most varied applications of scientific principles to the needs of human life— nay, of industries concerned with our daily subsistence. The same may be said of Cohn, whose researches into Bacteriology were begun in a purely theoretical study of botany; or of Lister's application of these general biological results to antisepsis. Nay, it would be easy to show how the thoroughness of such theoretical work on micro-organisms has directly influenced brewing and many other industries, besides advancing agriculture in all its ramifications. But the main point to bear in mind is: that it is inconceivable how any amount of technical work in brewing, in industrial or agricultural chemistry, could by itself have produced the "practical and material" results which commerce and industries now exploit. These were only achieved by the concentration of all intellectual power, in a strictly scientific method, on pure theory, without any thought of practical application. One small outcome of the stupendous theoretical work of the great chemist Bunsen is the "Bunsen burner," known to nearly every artisan. I venture to say that, without the establishment of the theoretical principle therein involved, the main factors underlying the development of locomotion in the motor-car, as well as many other practical results, would never have been attained. Professor Ewing informs me that his researches which led to the establishment of the property of *hysteresis* in metals (now in direct use and constant application by manufacturers of metal and engineers), were the result of purely theoretical work with no immediate apprehension of its practical use even after it was made. I wonder what the giant in pure mathematics, Gauss (who made the famous toast: " I drink to Pure Mathematics, the only science which has never been polluted by a practical application"), would think of the practical application of his *Methode der Kleinsten Quadrate*; or Laplace, were he to see the results of his work on the Doctrine of Probabilities. in daily application in the offices of actuaries and Life Insurance Companies.

I could continue page after page to give striking illustrations, which would all show how the most momentous and practical inventions of "Science" were either directly made by the pursuit of research in its highest and purest theoretical form, or, at least, could not have been made unless based upon such work. I could show that the life of "Science" upon which the material prosperity of a nation depends, can only be advanced, can only progress into the dim regions of the unknown and unachieved, through the conscientious labour of individuals who make up what constitutes a real university, who realize and maintain its spirit.

But in view of the pressure of actual life and of the clamour of ignorant popular opportunism, it is no easy task to maintain this spirit of pure science and learning, both for the individual "professors" of such a high vocation, and for the institutions which ought to be their natural home—the universities. The temptations and allurements of material, mercenary reward are often too great for the man of science, and the insinuation of the immediately "technical" spirit into the universities is the rock ahead in their course of beneficent action for the nation and the world at large.

It requires the supreme effort of self-possession, the constant presence of the living ideals, enforced upon the workers by the atmosphere of the universities supported by the government and by public opinion, to produce effective scientific work, and to maintain this efficiency, upon which even the ultimate material well-being of the whole community depends. The premature intrusion of secondary application, of practical and economic use, into any scientific inquiry is likely to prove fatal to its fruitful termination. The standard and test of the value of higher academic work are in no way to be this "application."

If anything, it is wiser to adhere to Gauss's paradox—it will in the aggregate prove to be more practical and profitable to the national life as a whole. The chairs of pure mathematics and of Sanscrit are to be regarded as equally important and equally worthy of honour and support as the chairs of mechanics and agricultural chemistry.

It is in the interest of the nation that these high and pure ideals of a university, as above all the impersonal centre of the nation's striving after truth, be maintained—nay, that by the action of the government, of munificent patrons, and of the whole public, they be enforced and be diffused and made familiar among the population itself. Life will then take cognizance of Science to the advancement of both.

I have endeavoured in the above merely to impress the most important, the essential one, among the ideals which a university implies; and I have, moreover, impressed this chiefly by insisting upon its bearings on actual life, especially the economic aspect of life. When such an ideal is developed and ensured in a university, technical training and technical institutions, no doubt of deep importance to the nation, will derive inspiration from the universities and will be all the more efficient. Without such ideals, however, I doubt whether technical training will be of great or lasting advantage.

Extract from *The Study of Art in Universities*, London and
New York, 1896, pp. 51 seq., Harper & Bros.

APPENDIX II.

SCIENCE AND EMPIRICISM, THEORY AND PRACTICE

It is not needful for me to show to this audience the justification of universities in this highest sense in terms of practical life. It can easily be done, and has frequently had capable expositors. But I feel that in our time of popularization, of the direct appeal to popular approval for all higher intellectual efforts, it ought, perhaps, to be done more than ever[1]. The cry for direct encouragement of our industries through technical schools and all other means, the reorganization and spread of our elementary schools throughout the country, the extension of higher teaching, causes the voices of some friends of popular education to be raised to such a pitch in clamouring for its just requirements, that the tone of their appeals assumes the character of anger, until it loses itself in a protest against those forms of study and education which are not immediately responsive to these general demands. But the louder and more urgent these appeals grow, and the more they may strike a sympathetic chord in our own breasts, the more ought we to insist upon maintaining in its highest form of purity the spirit which guides the truly scientific work of universities. We may almost be justified in emphasizing this spirit in the form of a paradox. The well-known toast of the famous mathematician, Gauss, will bear repetition that may be instructive: "I drink," he said, "to Pure Mathematics, the only science which has never been *defiled* by practical application." In so far, pure mathematics are the most complete exposition of university study.

[1] See Note C, p. 188.

As regards the justification of such pursuits in life, they respond to a primary instinct of man, namely, his desire to know; and it is enough for us to say, in the first instance, that as this primary instinct in man is in no way harmful or unsocial, it is worthy of satisfaction and encouragement. And it is right that institutions should exist which are meant directly and in their chief purpose to satisfy and encourage this primary instinct in its purest form. And if we leave individual man and go to the social community as a whole, we find that, in the interest of the community taken collectively, it is right that there should be one centre, devoted exclusively to the search after truth for its own sake, to make this common life complete; as in the life of each household every side is arranged according to the natural tasks governing it: the considerations of profession, health, amusement, reading, thought; and as in the life of every individual man, each one of his faculties ought to have adequate exercise and play to maintain complete normality and health.

But, of course, it is all a question of proportion. The question, namely, of how much time and energy are individually or collectively to be devoted to each side. And with regard to the claims which the universities have in the common life of civilized communities, it is fair to consider, how great their claims are in comparison with other educational institutions, especially the elementary schools. It is needless to say, for instance, that in a community which is just entering into the stage of higher civilization, and in which the school system has not as yet been developed, so that its citizens are ignorant of the rudiments of necessary learning for the purposes of civilized communication, commerce and industry, it would be unwise to begin with the higher university education until the elementary schools which minister to the most general intellectual needs of the people have been thoroughly organized. Elementary schools respond to the common needs of daily life and are therefore essential to it, and they apply to all citizens equally. Not so, it is maintained, universities. Therefore the schools are much more necessary, and it is but right that they should be much more widespread than universities. But, granting this, and, in consequence, repelling all undue claims of higher education where they may conflict with those of schools, *nobody* would deny the right, nay, the necessity of encouraging the highest theoretical study within its due proportion in the community. It might then be said by the opponent of highest university study, the exaggerated practical man, that the use of such highest study being comparatively small, its direct and tangible bearings upon the immediate practical wants of the mass of the community being restricted, its claims should be in due proportion repressed. But even he will admit that there ought in every civilized country to be some place or places where, to say the least, this side of human nature should be satisfied and developed, without which the community would not be perfectly organized and completely equipped as a body at the height of modern culture. However much we may restrict its local habitation, it ought to satisfy this theoretical craving in the *purest form*, most directly and completely, that is, without alien or ulterior motives and aims. It is more urgent for the welfare of the community to have lighthouses and meteorological stations than to have astronomical observatories. But if we have several hundred lighthouses and stations, we may well have one observatory. And in this due proportion of 1 to 200, we may say that the observatory is as necessary to our life as are the lighthouses and stations. Nor will it be wise to vitiate and lower the spirit of the astronomer by modifying his thought and action in the direction of the practical functions of the other officials.

And for the moment accepting this almost paradoxical limitation of the function of a university, I would then distinguish it from the ordinary schools, in that its primary aim is not educational but theoretical and scientific; whereas the primary aim of schools is educational and not in the first instance theoretical or scientific. And in so far as they are both educational bodies, I would say that a university becomes educational, because it is scientific; and a school must be scientific because it is educational. I could easily show how ultimately this concentration upon theoretical aims on the part of universities will prove most practical in their relation not only to general education, but also to the most material aspects of public life[1].

In this sense I have viewed universities chiefly as the homes of research, as bodies which are intrusted by the community with the highest interests of pure science which they are directly to further and, by the collective efforts of its working members to advance, keeping pace with the progress made by the whole community in civilization and general life.

While maintaining this spirit they will best be able to turn their energies to account when they flow into the broader educational channels. The university teacher ought always to be a researcher himself, and however much he may consider it his duty to further the education of the students who put themselves under his guidance as a teacher, he ought to do it in the spirit of a researcher. But the objection may be made, and has frequently been made, that we shall then only train specialists and only teach in the spirit of specialists[2]. My answer to this is, that it is right that we should do this even from the point of view of general education. It stands to reason, nay, it is almost a platitude to say that one who wishes to devote his life to some special study or profession must learn his subject as thoroughly as possible, which means as a specialist. But even those who do not wish to apply the knowledge they may gain at the university in the direct channels of the subject they there pursue, even for those the education which they receive in this spirit of pure theoretical and scientific knowledge and the methods of thought and of work which are inculcated in them through any study followed systematically, cannot but be of the highest advantage.

[1] See Note D, p. 191.

[2] I can only say that to listen to the stammering of a Helmholtz or a Ranke would be more impressive and instructive than to hear the most perfect oratory of a popularizer of physics or history. The personality of the men, whom we know to be the leaders and advancers of their own science in the world, to which they have conscientiously devoted their lives, is an educational vehicle which cannot be over-estimated. So also I think the reading of a book like Huxley's *Crayfish* will convey more insight into Biology than any general popular treatise.

First, it can only be pure gain to any man that in the course of his career he should for one short period of his existence live in this purely intellectual atmosphere, and that he should acquire the scientific habit of mind, the power of co-ordinating facts, the habit of following causality to its earliest stages, and the faculty of careful observation and of complete concentration of mind. To turn these methods into life, to make them a part of his very consciousness is no small gain. And in order that the student should reap these advantages to the fullest degree it is necessary that the teacher should himself be imbued with the exclusively theoretical spirit of investigation, that he should not be influenced by the practical considerations of the life which, by an act of sympathy, he may prescribe in the future to the students who are before him. Nay, even the immediate practical issues, such as the examinations which the students may have to pass, may dilute or perturb the purity of the spirit which is to permeate his every effort as an educator.

We, university teachers, know the dangers arising out of this thraldom of examinations, which, however useful and necessary they may be as tests and as stimuli, still act as degrading and vitiating to the spirit of our teaching when we admit of their undue intrusion into our academic instruction. And in the arrangement and organization of our courses of study we must be careful lest the pressure which comes from without, the desire of intellectually cutting our coat according to the cloth, lead us to compromise with the claims of the would-be practical life. I remember a phrase of a German *savant* which impressed me much at the time. He warned us against what he called *Die Wissenschaft auf dem Präsentierteller*, which reminds me of the story of the lady in a French *salon*[1]. We cannot turn the uni-

---

[1] I am reminded of this story told by the late George Henry Lewes. The scene was laid in a brilliant Parisian *salon*, where an eminent French man of science was conversing with the hostess, a *spirituelle*, though thoroughly worldly, society-lady. He possessed that child-like simplicity and sincerity which often mark the truly great man; and thus he was deceived by the tone of intense interest which she adopted when asking him (to make conversation) about some law of nature (say, the conservation of energy) which was just then being

versity into a great culinary institution in which scientific dishes
are prepared and cooked to suit the palates and the digestions
of all the different professional candidates. We rob them of one
of the greatest educational advantages, namely, the *search* after
the intellectual food itself which will cause them to grow up as
strong and efficient men, ready to cope with all the varied and
unforeseen difficulties of life, instead of effeminate, narrow-
chested sybarites who can only thrive under the conditions in
which they have been brought up in their provincial home. We
cannot prepare a small dose of physiological study for the
student of medicine, just enough to suffice him for his service
at the sick bed; but we can send him to the most thorough
physiologist, such as we have here, and, without waste of time,
he can there drink in pure scientific information at the fountain-
head of real research. We cannot extract from history, that is
to say from the development of man in the past, those facts
which may be useful for the training of the future statesman,
thereby caricaturing history and enfeebling the mind of this
future prime minister. But we can for once in his life, lead him
to concentrate all his energies upon thorough knowledge, and
we can increase his fund of accurate information and strengthen
his power of thinking rightly. So, too, in dealing with art in a
university, the student must clearly hold before his mind this
purely theoretical aim, ignoring all others: to know and only to
know.

much discussed. The *savant*, delighted with this sign of interest on
the part of a woman whom he had considered frivolous, entered upon
a lucid exposition of the main principles, and was so much wrapt up
in his subject, that he did not notice how her eyes were wandering
about the room. But he was pulled up short when she asked, with a
touch of *naïve* coquetry: "*Mais est-ce bien vrai, ça, monsieur?*" He
at once drew himself up and, with a deep bow, turning both hands to
his breast, he said: "*Parole d'honneur, madame !*"

NOTE C

(O.C. pp. 118 seq.)

Indifference to Scientific Pursuits in England.

It has often been maintained that the English people are naturally opposed to such theoretical study, that they have a practical bias, and that they have a dislike to, if not a contempt for, abstract speculation and pure theory, which goes with their craving for the concrete. This aversion to speculation may possibly be racial. But I doubt this. One need merely quote the Germans, who are our next of kin, and in whom the love of speculation and of theoretical science has been most highly developed, to confirm this doubt. Nor should I even believe that this is a national characteristic of the British people; for one may at once point to the Scotch, who have been marked for the widespread interest which they take in subjects of philosophical speculation. I may at once say that this difference between the English and the Scotch may be accounted for by one circumstance in the moral development of the two peoples, which may, in its turn, contribute to the understanding of the problem before us. It is to be found in the different religious history of the two peoples. The English have had an established church, while the Scotch people are largely made up of those who have had to fight for, or to fight out in themselves, their religious opinions. As this struggle on the part of a truly "protestant" people will develop the speculative and abstract mood, even when applied to other subjects, so a formally established church with its doctrines will lead to a comparative indifference, if not an aversion, to such speculation—at all events, it does not encourage it. In the whole history of thought in all times and climes there has been an early religious stage to the study of pure science and philosophy.

One has often heard the complaint raised by English representatives of pure science, of the lack of real interest in their efforts on the part of the people; and by the people they are far from meaning the *populus*, or the masses, but they include "the classes "; in fact, the various movements and associations among the labouring classes have to a great degree stimulated the interests of these people in matters of thought. The complaint is made in the universities also, that there is little widespread interest in the higher university studies; and even in the universities themselves for what is called research. I believe this complaint is justified to a considerable degree; but I do not think it essential to the English people, but accidental. We might here again point to Scotland and to the United States of America, which differ from us in this point, and which therefore go far to prove the accidental nature of this feature.

Among these causes I think the most important the peculiar nature of school and university education in England. In the first place, there have been, and even are now, fewer complete universities in England than in other countries similarly situated abroad. The result is that, in spite of the few great personalities which England has always produced and which stand out as the most marked luminaries on the horizon of science, there is not a large and important body of such workers, sufficiently large to be recognized by the near-sighted mass of the people, and thus in a rough and ready way to impress them with the importance and stability of such pursuits[1]. In the eyes of the people science has not yet risen to the standing of a profession.

Our school education, so far from encouraging reverence or love for scientific work, tends to lower it in the eyes of the boys. The ideals are essentially unintellectual. There is very little done positively to develop this enthusiasm among the boys; while the widespread interest in sport and games, and the unquestioned ascendancy which these have as standards of excellence and distinction among the boys, go far to repress still more any claim of prestige on the part of the intellectual pursuits. I am the last to ignore the inestimable value of athletic

[1] One of my colleagues was talking to a German professor on the difference between England and Germany. The Herr Professor asked: "In England you have no *class* of learned men, have you?" "O yes," replied my friend, "we have." "But how do you call them?" "*Wir nennen sie* 'prigs,'" was his reply.

games in the development of English character, but I quote it here in its negative effects upon popular estimation of science.

As the games act at school, so, in later life, the ascendancy of politics over other liberal vocations acts in the same way. Not only that the interest which attaches to political activity is supreme and is conducive to prestige, and that, in so far, it draws heavily on the rising talent, which might in other countries be directed towards scientific pursuits; but, at the same time, and, perhaps, because of this, it tends to lower the standing of scientific men as a body or class.

But there seems to me a more direct, though less evident, cause for this want of appreciation and enthusiasm. It is to be found in the prize-system of schools and universities. The number of prizes and scholarships existing in the schools and universities of England is quite unparalleled in any other country. They have long since drifted far away from the original purpose of supporting the studies of those who are in actual need, and they have, in the first instance, been only used as means of creating more intense emulation and competition. The "scholars" of our great public schools and of many of the colleges in our universities are far from being the children of poor parents; and, though many may not be rich, still I venture to say that there is but a very small proportion who are in dire need of such support. It has gone so far, that schools and colleges, perhaps unconsciously, and not directly and avowedly, seem to bid against one another for talented candidates for instruction; and that these candidates themselves, even at an early age, are put in a position of choosing the highest bidder, and of recognizing their own value in accepting—the great boon of being allowed to learn.

The result is that, at a very early age, the enthusiasm is not only not awakened, but is stunted in its growth or entirely eradicated. The boy and the young man have enforced upon them the recognition that the act of learning is to be paid for and has its market value. The result again is (as I have been able to appreciate by comparison with students of other countries), that, in spite of the excellent men we breed in these homes of learning, there is a comparative want of enthusiasm among them, an absence of that deep gratitude which glows in the eyes and comes from the heart of the students I have seen in Germany and America and in Scotland at being allowed to drink in information at the very fountain-head. I feel a general bluntness which can best be expressed by the French word *blasé*.

This I ascribe entirely to the system of scholarships as it now exists. I will not here refer to the material disadvantages of this system, when we consider how large a proportion of the incomes of our schools and universities (now cramped for means of developing their teaching) are devoted to this fungus growth in the fields of charity running to seed. But I will finally point to the further harmful influence of this condition as affecting the parents, and, through them, the general interest in science on the part of the people. With a large number of those who have benefited by such subvention, it has robbed them of the wholesome feeling of sacrifice which they would otherwise make to secure the advantages of education for their children; and it has caused them, as it did the boys themselves, to look upon education, not as a privilege, but as a matter the acceptance of which requires pay as an inducement. In so far their minds have been diverted from the end of education as a thing of supreme value in itself, and, in consequence, they can never rise into the pure and abstract regions where learning and science are spiritual goods which have their standard and value in themselves.

NOTE D

(O. C. pp. 126 seq.)

Dangers to Industry arising out of Empiricism. I have been told by manufacturers and representatives of technical industries abroad that England was losing the supremacy which natural advantages (such as coal and minerals) and practical ingenuity had given her in the past; while countries like Germany, Switzerland, and even Italy, were making rapid advances. I believe this is chiefly due to the fact that

England is too much bound down by empiricism. Empiricism is a very good thing, and produces excellent results where there is great wealth of natural resources, and unhampered opportunities without the pressure of time in active competition. Could we each of us live through many lives and generations for a thousand years with our eyes and ears open, we might gain experience and wisdom more effectively than is conveyed to us by much teaching and much reading. But when the natural resources dwindle, and the pressure of time grows, when we are pressed out of the favourable position of easy monopoly into one of severe competition, empiricism will not suffice to secure the retention of our advantage. Then practice must be strengthened, advanced, and hastened in its advance, by well matured and applied theory. I would almost like to venture upon a comprehensive aphorism, and to say: that progress in civilization means the closer approximation between theory and practice, law and conduct. And I believe that the stress in this approximation is not to be put upon the modification of theory in accordance with practice; but, rather, in the directness, vividness, and facility with which practice makes use of, and is effected by, theory. "Technical Schools" of a popular character are not the panacea to our industrial ailments. The best chemist for a specific manufactory, the most versatile mechanic, the most thorough, and, in so far, the most efficient electrician for industrial purposes, the physician and practitioner who is least likely to be baffled by turns in diseases that diverge from the ordinary course, are not those who have been trained "technically" and empirically for the immediate tasks which their craft is supposed to lay upon them; but they have come from a university (and this is generally the case in German factories) where they have learnt the fundamental principles of their science and of all science; where, *for a time*, they have concentrated all their faculties upon the task of grasping the very core and essence of their branch of study in theory. At all events, such a man has gained the *scientific* spirit, which for him will mean (when he has turned to active pursuits) the greatest power to overcome the immediate checks to his plans or experiments, to go deeper down to the fundamental causes of failures and successes in the phenomena he produces, induces, or which present themselves to him, and hence to multiply and vary his resources and devices—to apply his own hard common sense, supported by the very principles of things and by common sense of innumerable people before him. This is the case in Germany; but it is not universally the case in England.

Reprinted from *The Journal of Education*, June, 1916.

APPENDIX III.

EDUCATIONAL REFORM

A most important issue has been raised by the two manifestos published in *The Times* of May 4—the one by Sir E. Ray Lankester's Committee, the other by a number of representative men of learning and culture, including some specialists of the natural sciences. The proposals they contain are vital to our national life, in the present and for the future. A false step, a hasty reform, or a complete revolution of our educational system, might prove fatal to our national life for generations to come. But the opinions expressed by both parties are in no way unreasonable or extreme, and can surely be reconciled. Is it too much to hope that the two bodies will meet and co-operate, and, if possible, found a great Educational Reform League to improve our national education? Would it not be possible for them, thus united, to seek for and to confirm—not the differences in their views—which have already been abundantly formulated, but the points of agreement which they could bring before the administrative authorities with weight of influence ensuring practical realization?

If Sir E. Ray Lankester's Committee were to succeed in securing more complete recognition for the study of modern languages and, especially, for instruction in the principles and achievements of the natural sciences, they will have done a great service to the nation. On the other hand, they must effectually guard against the fatal misconception in the teaching of these subjects—a misconception which is almost inevitable, if not in their own case, at all events among the wider public— that they are to be taught with a view to producing the specialist or technical journeyman. The wider teaching of science must be humanistic in nature, in which even the most technical and utilitarian studies are ultimately—and even immediately—pursued in what we must call the humanistic spirit.

The aims of such teaching are to be the training of thought and taste, the development and refinement of the sense of truth, the increase of knowledge; they are not to be affected by the premature introduction of "applied" and opportunistic ends. We must all admit that no man is properly educated (may I use the word "cultured"?) whatever his classical, historical, literary, or artistic attainments, who has not imbibed the spirit of modern science and has not some acquaintance with its achievements.

It is not enough to know Shakespeare; we must also know Newton if we claim to have grasped the history and meaning of English civilization. On the other hand, from the point of view of national education, it must be admitted that the *Principia* are not to the same degree accessible and intelligible to all people as are the works of Shakespeare, because they only represent one aspect of human life—its thought and its needs— while Shakespeare covers the wholeness of human life; the subject-matter and the language necessarily appeal to all, and his work thus forms part of what have justly been called the *humanistic* studies. In the case of Hellenic or classical literature, this applies to all Western nations. The classics will thus always form the groundwork of general education.

No man recognized this more fully than the late A. W. v. Hoffmann, the great scientific chemist of the past generation of German educationists, who helped to lay the foundation of that purely scientific organization which has been applied to German industries, and even to the conduct of war. In his Rectorial Address at the University of Berlin, delivered many years ago, he maintained with great clearness of conviction and exposition that the classical education in the *Gymnasia* of the Germany of old was ultimately productive of higher standards of scientific research and achievement, and immediately of better men to further its ends, than the teaching of what we call "the modern side." The result of the spirit of his teaching and of that of his scientific colleagues (to adhere to only the one instance of Hoffmann's work) has been that the aniline industry (though discovered in England by Perkin, under whom Hoffmann worked) has been monopolized by Germany. The three factories which thus control that industry (at Mannheim, Hoechst, and Elberfeld), besides their armies of workmen, have each about 350 highly trained scientific chemists, most of them educated in the purest spirit of their science in universities, and not in technical schools. One hundred of these may be occupied in direct supervision and management, while two hundred are engaged in more remote chemical research in the same spirit and with the same methods as prevail in higher research in universities. I am, on the other hand, told that the largest chemical works in the United Kingdom employ at most ten highly trained chemists.

Now what does this mean? Not that 350 highly trained chemists flocked to the doors of the factory to dump their unsolicited intellectual merchandise before ignorant and recalcitrant employers, but that these employers—and the nation at large—were sufficiently well educated to realize the advantage of pure science and research; that they called for such scientific assistance, and gradually developed their extensive research laboratories, which ultimately were turned to such enormous commercial profit. It certainly does not mean that we ought to concentrate our energies on the technical training of chemical or other scientific journeymen, but that, as a nation, we must fight what Meredith called "England's hatred of thought"— the general mistrust of the expert. We must not listen to the clamour of the popular sciolist, that we ought to level science and education *down* to the needs of our industrial and commercial life, but we must raise the nation up to the understanding and appreciation of the highest science, even the abstract and humanistic aspect of it. This will lead to thoroughness in its application to the varied needs of the nation and of its economic life.

One truth it is, however, most important for us to remember at the present moment:

That the success attained by Germany in its industrial and commercial development during the last forty years, as well as in its preparation for this War, and where it has been legitimately successful in the waging of it, is entirely due to the infusion of the spirit of thoroughness into the whole German nation by such men of the previous generation as v. Hoffmann, by Virchow and Helmholtz, Gauss, Kirchhof, and Bunsen, and innumerable representatives of humanistic studies kindred in spirit with these; that these men were all trained in "classical" schools; and that this humanistic spirit of those former days, affecting the life of the whole nation, was again the inheritance of the thought derived from their philosophic predecessors, such as Kant, Fichte, Schelling, Hegel. Out of this inherited earlier spirit has come the thoroughness and the appreciation of scientific organization in the functions of the government, as well as the appreciation of things of the mind on the part of the whole people. I have endeavoured to show elsewhere how this monstrous War is the result of the rise and dominance of *Strebertum*, the victory of the modern "pusher," the very antithesis of the traditions of the older Germany. I maintained that, in so far as the older spirit has survived, Germany are successful, and that all that is bad and leads to their ultimate undoing, as it has already produced the moral degeneration of the German people, is due to the new *Alldeutsches Strebertum*.

It is in the nature of these hasty, intellectual *parvenus* to exaggerate the importance of the application of science to military organization. By a curious paradox they become the pedants who build up theories of national psychology, and imagine that systematic frightfulness will overcome the nerve of highly intelligent, as well as healthy and sturdy, enemies. It is they who place their chief hope on Zeppelins and submarines and on superior railway organization. On the other hand, the War will be won by the Allies the more rapidly as they increase the thorough and scientific organization of the business of war, while retaining the moral qualities which, as nations, they possess. We must free ourselves from the mistrust or the neglect of the expert which leads our Government to assign skilled work to unskilled amateurs, and produces instances such as that quoted by Lord Montagu—instances which can be multiplied a hundredfold. But we must go deeper and wider than this until we come to the prevalent ideals of education, where, with the exception of the Scottish people (whose appreciation of thought and learning is comparatively high), the general value placed upon intellectual achievement and eminence is of the lowest. So long as the nation at large (from the governing classes, through the employers of labour and the labourers themselves) does not justly appreciate such moral values, there is little hope of improvement. But, above all, when the parents in their homes—however priceless our national sports are to us—prefer their sons to gain distinction in the world of sport or in social eminence rather than as able scholars, and even encourage contempt for intellectual achievements, the best educational systems and the efforts of all our pedagogues will be in vain. And yet, recognizing the crying need for reform in the teaching and efficient diffusion of culture and of science, let us always retain our national ideals of manhood as conveyed by the term " gentleman "—the man possessed of culture, including the understanding and the appreciation of the natural sciences as well as the humanities, the man delighting in our sports and our outdoor life, with the accompanying spirit of fair-play, chivalry, and generous manliness. For "the man's the gowd for a' that"—and it's the man who wins wars.

Reprinted from *Harper's Weekly*, Aug. 16, 1890.

APPENDIX IV.

MODESTY

My friend J. R. is one of the profoundest thinkers I have ever met. He has done more original research in his own line of work, has contributed more to widen the sphere of the known, to fix and define and complete what was before but imperfectly known, than any man in England. Besides this, he is a most widely read and accomplished man, full of attainments which make life interesting and profitable, appreciative not only of everything that is great and beautiful and good, but even of what is pretty and graceful and amusing. These attainments that others consciously strive for, and when possessed after much effort are always aware of, were part of his whole nature, and seemed to be spontaneous outpourings of his personality. With him the answer to the question "Can you play the violin?" —"I do not know; I have never tried"—almost lost its humorous point, for really it looked as if he might have done everything he desired to do, if only he tried it.

With all this he is the man of the most healthful modesty, free from all shyness and free from all pride. He is free from shyness, on the one hand, because he is intellectually (and perhaps, therefore, also emotionally) free from selfishness, because he is not thinking always of himself and the way he may strike others or the way they may treat him, and is interested in and engrossed by the people he meets and the things he is discussing or contemplating. On the other hand, he is not proud, because his standard of self-estimation is not based upon a comparison of his own merits and advantages with those of others, and he is thus not aware of or interested in the superiority he may possess over others; nor is he diffident from constantly looking for and discovering points of inferiority in himself as compared with his neighbour. He has no such vacillating, mean, and unhealthy standards. His standards for judging other people, or for appreciating work and things, are *outside* himself, free from egotistical bias; his standards for judging himself are *within* himself, in the ideals of perfection or perfectibility, which stimulate his every effort, and are the grounds for self-commendation or esteem, or self-distrust or reproof.

I have never met a man so free from envy or jealousy, so joyously upraised by the discovery of virtue or skill or strength in other men, of beauty and goodness and brilliancy in women, of merit and genius in work. Nay, this extends to a natural faculty for discovering a humorous point in a simple tale, or a humble incident, of seeing quaintness in an object approaching the grotesque, of finding fun in a mishap that would otherwise sour the temper of a whole party. His appreciation of nature is marked by the same healthful unselfishness. He cannot understand the narrowness of appreciation of those who grumble at a flat country because they like mountains. His catholicity of taste leads him to say: "Give me a hayrick and a hedge and a bit of green turf on the roadside, with a purplish or buff ploughed field beyond, a bit of sunlight, a bit of blue haze, a cloud or two, and the delight in its way is as great as when the Matterhorn at sunset fills one's soul with awe."

The same charitable disposition (really charitable, because it is unconscious of its charity or of any attribute of itself) pervades his treatment of other men. He somehow or other cannot help seeing a good or interesting point in people in whom we only saw what is bad or dull; and to these points he would cling in dealing with them or thinking of them. And thus he had friends and friendly acquaintances among all manner of men, even among those of whom many of us disapproved: the brainless riding man ("rattling good sort, straight sporty fellow, a jolly plucky man, that!"); the priggish sulky learned man ("X was quite talkative this evening, he is really doing first-class work, his is the real stuff"); the smuggish bore ("I hardly know a purer-hearted man than Y; he has got rid of that beastly tie and looked quite a swell to-day")—he found something nice in them all, and they really became good fellows when with him; he would not give them an opportunity to show

their disagreeable side. I remember one day finding him in one
of his moods of deepest blues. These generally came when his
numerous occupations and duties grew too much for him; when,
with a hopeless accumulation of things he felt he ought to do,
he sat in almost despair, folding his hands and feeling that he
could do nothing at all. Sometimes a jar upon his sensitiveness,
something "ugly and base" would strike the keynote and
throw him into this dismal mood for days. Not unfrequently
this oppression of work was caused by the fact that his social
disposition and his power of attracting people preyed upon
his time and energy to such an extent that his work
would suffer by it. He would then, in this frame of morbid
relaxation, burst forth in a fit of bitter self-depreciation, gibe
at himself, his self-indulgence, want of method, and general
good-for-nothingness. Toward the end of one of these fits, he
suddenly turned upon me, one day, and said: "Smith said
something to me and about me the other day which pleased me
more than I can tell you. I wonder whether it is true? If it is,
I have some reason, after all, to be satisfied with myself. You
know, we have been great friends for years, but have not seen
much of each other for some time. He came up to stay with me
last week, and we compared notes of our past selves as if we
were dead. 'One thing of you has remained foremost in my
mind,' he said. 'You always make people show their best side
to you. A man can't be a brute when being with you or thinking
of you. And they do this without coquetry, or lying, until
gradually that nicer side may grow biggest in them.' That
would indeed be a splendid quality to possess. I wonder
whether I really have it? Perhaps I have."

He had a favourite parable which he found somewhere in
Goethe. He used to quote it not only because of its contents,
but because he considered it a model of the literary form of
parable, namely, one in which the truth conveyed was pithily
couched in the very strongest contrasts—in this case, pure
beauty and the putrefying carcass of a dog. It ran: "And the
Lord was walking with his disciples. And they came upon the
carcass of a dog which was rotting in the sun. And one disciple
held his eyes and said, 'What a sight!' And the other held his

nose and said, 'What a stench!' And the Lord spake, 'The
teeth are white as pearls!'"

I am afraid that I may have given the impression that my
friend was a prig. This would be absolutely wrong. He had
nothing of the sermonizer about him, and only dwelt upon these
more serious moral considerations when with intimate friends
or when the surrounding circumstances called for serious treatment. His definition of prig is most characteristic. Prig and
snob he maintained to be supplementary ideas. A prig, according to him, was in the intellectual sphere what a snob was
in the social sphere. I remember the interesting discussion we
had that evening which brought out his definition. It was at
the house of a very brilliant lady in London. We were discussing
one of the great writers of the day, when someone said, quite
lightly, "I think him a snob." We all felt a shock; and I over-
heard our hostess turning to our friend and saying "Have
you not always had a sneaking feeling that in applying that
word to any person you were something of it yourself?" There
was some danger of an embarrassed lull spreading over the
whole company. My friend's tact led him to the rescue. He
diverted the disturbing personal element into impersonal and
general channels, in recalling Thackeray's definition of a snob
and criticizing it. When pressed to attempt at defining a snob
himself, he pointed to the fact that snob and prig explained one
another, and defined a snob as "a person who was manifestly
and obtrusively conscious of his social advantages or disadvantages; a prig was the same in the sphere of intellect and morals."
A duke, or even a king, who was thus manifestly conscious of
his social advantage, and showed it in his actions and bearing,
was a snob, as much as a cobbler who thus manifested his social
deficiency. The browbeating professor, who flaunts his superior
knowledge in the face of all poor laymen, conscious of his
learning, is as much of a prig as the *famulus Wagner* who is
melting with his own ignorance in the light of his learned master
Faust. And the little Jack Horner, very good boy, who is so
constantly eating the plum of moral self-gratulation with sticky
fingers, is as much of a prig as the humble "sinner" whose back
is fairly broken under the weight of sins which he acknowledges

himself to have the merit of carrying. "I cannot stand the intellectually or morally *nouveau riche*," I have heard him say; "he is as bad and as self-assertive as the shoddy is in the social sphere." Good-breeding is good-breeding because it *is* and does not know it; and brains and heart are most there when they do not show their anatomy. It is only in disease or *post-mortems* that brains and hearts are worth studying as such. His type of a snob and a prig combined was the young Duke in Browning's *Flight of the Duchess*:

For what the old Duke was without knowing it,
The young Duke fain would know that he was without being it.

No, my friend was certainly not the prig or the good boy. He was very demonstrative of his displeasure when he felt it, and expressed it in strong language. Nor did his modesty prevent him from "jumping upon" people when he was convinced that they deserved it. He was once on a scientific commission which had met to decide some points that were much discussed at the time. At the first meeting he felt strongly that, whereas some definite questions could efficiently be studied and decided upon by the commission, there were the wider, general questions which did not admit of a final and direct solution by anybody at that time. He therefore moved a restriction of the ground to be covered, confessing that he was not able to form a satisfactory opinion owing to the absence of data for the formation of such an opinion. This ignorance he entirely ascribed to himself. But when one member of the commission, a man holding a great position in the world, and who (as my friend afterwards confessed to me) really knew less about the question in hand than he did, began patronizingly to assure him that he and other members would provide him with facts, his patience gave way, and, walking to the other end of the long table, he put his hand on the distinguished man's shoulder and said: "When I said that I did not know enough of the subject, I did not mean to imply that you did; my ignorance does not produce your knowledge; nor, gentlemen (turning to the whole assembly), do I mean to imply that any one of you here present, or any other body of men, is capable of deciding this question at the present state of the facts." He was greeted with applause and carried his point.

He loved to see "cocksureness" rebuked, and delighted in the snub which the late master of Trinity gave a dogmatic young man when he summed up the youthful orator's tirade: "Yes, we are none of us infallible, not even the youngest among us." On the other hand, no one irritated him as much at certain meetings, and led him to the use of such strong language, as a very distinguished and reverend scholar, who with a humility that was in bad taste, if not disingenuous, would always preface his remarks with phrases such as, "though I know less about this matter than you all here do," "though I have absolutely no right to an opinion" (though he was called upon by duty and position to have one), etc., etc. He often chuckled over "dear old B's" dogmatic rudeness. B was an old German professor, *facile princeps* in his own line of work. He would constantly confess that he had not given sufficient attention to one or the other departments of his study, and would listen with genuine interest and avidity of learning to what a younger member of his guild had to tell him. Scholars in the same branch passing through his university town, which lies in a much frequented district, would often meet there when setting out upon or returning from their holiday trip. In the evening all would meet at a beer-garden, and, under the presidency of old B there was much interesting "shop" talked. On one occasion, among the people thus assembled, was a very aggressive younger German professor, who, in a loud voice and a very disagreeable, thumping manner, was laying down the law. All present were much irritated with him, but it apparently had not yet moved the equanimity of mild old B. At last the rude young prig was holding forth loudly on a matter which happened to be a question of argument and not of fact, so that a discussion could well be maintained on his side. But his manner was so offensive that it roused even the modest old B. Turning round to the young professor, from the head of the table where he sat, he, with almost exaggerated quiet and solemnity, raised his fore-finger, which was long and bony, and, slowly waving it in pendulum fashion to and fro before the speaker's face, he said, quietly and solemnly: "*Nein, Herr Professor, das ist nicht so*" (No, Professor, that is not so). The argument was closed; there was nothing more to say, and nothing more was said, though there was much to be said. It was the only time modest old B had ever been seen dogmatic, the only time he seemed aware and conscious of his own dignity, and seemed to be resting his claim upon the works he had written so long ago, and to speak *ex cathedra* whence he had taught generations of scholars. It was the justified revolt of true modesty stung by arrogance.

Some time ago there came into our circle a very remarkable man, who was preceded by a reputation of extraordinary ability. He was tall and strong and dark, and of very striking appearance. The extent of his knowledge on all manner of subjects was phenomenal. He had travelled a great deal, seen and known all manner of people, had read widely and extensively, and astonished us all with his intimate familiarity with out-of-the-way facts of history and literature, of art and craft, of peoples and countries. He spoke in a quiet way, with great succinctness and directness, and did not hesitate to correct the slips of those who spoke vaguely or inaccurately on subjects. My friend was at once deeply impressed by him. "I have never met anybody like him. He makes me feel like mud. He does teach one humility. He makes me feel what a humbug I am. There I am skulking and sneaking through the world of thought with a pitiable, small, mean capital of facts and accurate knowledge, always drawing and overdrawing my poor account of facts to launch out into the greatest spheres of thought and speculation, living from hand to mouth, forced to refer to a book for the simplest, commonest fact, and that man has it all there, neatly stored away in his brain, ready to be referred to whether walking in the street, or smoking in a club, or chatting with a lady in a drawing-room. Do not tell me that this stupendous memory and wealth of facts are purchased at the expense of speculative faculty. I tried that sneaking, ungenerous, belittling prop to my tottering vanity; he can think fully as well as we can, though he knows so much more than we do, you cannot cling even to this last straw of self-conciliation. No, he is a wonderful man; I admire him very much, and shall love him very soon."

This burst of admiration was very characteristic of him. But soon I found that he did not speak so much of this wonderful polyhistor; he avoided talking about him, and would not express an opinion when he was discussed. One day at a dinner, when this wonderful man gave another evidence of unexpected, accurate knowledge, I was astonished to see our friend lean over, and, in his pleasant way, that made offence almost impossible, say: "S, I shall like you quite the first time I hear you say 'I don't know.'" As we walked home that evening, I, meaning to draw him, referred to the remarkable instance of universal information given by S that evening. "Well, I don't know," he simply said, "I have some vague memory of those facts, and I think he was quite out in his statement, though it was made with great weight and positiveness. I must look it up when I get back to my study." And when we arrived there, to smoke our last pipe before going to bed, he at once put his hand upon a fat volume, and, frowning, he said dryly, "Yes, I was quite right; S is quite out of it."

From that day I noticed traces of irritation in our friend (very uncommon with him) whenever he was in the presence of the great S. Some months after this he rushed into my room one evening, and began to talk rapidly, walking up and down, as was his wont when excited, "I can't stand it—I am bursting with rage. I have had it pent up now for months, until my nerves are tingling with it. I have had it out with S like a stupid school-boy, and what I am especially sorry for is that I was rude to him in my own rooms. I wish I had not done it there: I have old-fashioned views on hospitality and such things. But, hang it, it was all true, deeply true, and I could not help saying it! Please, my dear fellow, discount from the violence of diction of what I say now, I do not really mean it all so strongly; but it relieves me to shout it out, and I wish the world could hear it—for it is so true, so true.

"You know how I began by admiring S for his wonderful information. But he soon puzzled me. I began to feel that he must be made quite differently from myself, was built on quite a different scale to feel things in so final a shape, to be so serene amidst the puzzling maze of things. I was quite prepared to look upon myself as an utter fool (fool that I was for doing so) until a slight circumstance gave me the first shock. I told him one day of a new German dissertation containing some interesting discoveries which I had just received, and gave him a short superficial account of its contents. I promised to lend it to him in a few days, when I could spare it. The very next day, by a curious chance, the subject dealt with in this dissertation was referred to in hall. After several of those present gave cautious views, S with that quiet, self-contained, and oracular finality, gave the few poor superficial facts I had told him as a weak summary of the German's work the day before, as a wonderful and striking ray of light amidst the tenebrous groping of hesitating opinion. The setting the words had on his lips, the conviction and maturity of personal assimilation, pointing to years of thought and experience which they seemed to possess from his personality, made it all sound so differently, that I doubted whether they really were the facts which I had cast before him in a hasty conversation the previous day. Now, there is nothing wrong in using information but recently acquired because its acquisition has been recent. But the tone in which this was conveyed was misleading; it pointed to an intimate acquaintance with the whole subject which I knew him not to possess; it promised so much more behind the mere words spoken. I received a shock which, for the first time, made me doubt him, and I could not help watching for confirmation of my suspicions. From that moment I continually found him making assertions with that simple dignified assurance which were quite unfounded. I realized that his great effort was to hide his ignorance and to shine with his knowledge. He is eaten up by vanity, nurtured by the fatal frailty of his memory, and by the wonderment and admiration of the people whom he thus impresses, until it has become a powerful stimulus for which he craves like a drunkard, eating away the moral vitality and sensibility, which, from the traces which have not yet been obliterated, he must have possessed to a high degree. He has no reverence for the heroic effort it costs to master the whole truth; he cannot feel the great thrill of grasping her in one's arms in all her purity after one has fought one's way through the night and storm of doubt, the toils of puzzling fallacies, and the enemies of light. Nay, it has gone farther and has eaten at his heart. He fears discovery, like an impostor, and as he deals lightly with facts and things, he deals lightly with human beings and their character. It sounded as captivating in its boldness and directness to hear him praise one man as the greatest of his kind, and condemn others as the worst and basest. Well, he had no justification for passing judgment upon people whose works and life he barely knew, using his personal impressiveness (itself a sham) to extol or demolish another man in the eyes of all who come within its influence. I hear that he praises me. I *will* not be praised by him; it is an insult to me. He is a bad man, whose judgment is guided by selfishness and vanity as much as is that of a child or a thoughtless girl. Were he either of these it would not strike me so. He came this evening really to ask for information; but he could not bring himself to ask it simply. His questions came in the form of information given to me. I could stand it no longer; my pent-up wrath burst out, and I told him how vicious I considered that habit of mind.

"Oh, my dear fellow, how I hate it! How one ought to preach against it! We civilized Europeans feel the gulf of difference that lies between ourselves and the African savage, between our moral standards and those of the Oriental. Well, I say that those of us who have cultivated this sense of the sanctity of truth, and of the supreme claims of just thought, are different beings, live in a different moral world, from those whose sense in this direction is blunted or has remained in embryo. A sense is wanting in them, and that sense is fundamental in its power of guiding us rightly in the complicated organization of our social life; it has become necessary to us, as cardinal a virtue, as the law against stealing and murdering was to a simpler and earlier stage of civilization. Why, we can divide educated society into two groups; those who possess this virtue, and those who do not.

"But what is most astonishing is the fact, how many people of refined moral sensibility there are among us who are entirely blunt as regards the appreciation of this cardinal virtue. They

shrink with horror from any of the grosser vices, they refuse
their hand to any person convicted of what they call lying, and
they do not see that this is lying, the more dangerous and destructive because not recognized as a vicious disease, under-
mining the moral constitution of individuals, of classes, and of
society. How often does a man distinguished in art or fiction or
politics lay down the law upon some question of science, to
which men with great initial power of thought have devoted
their whole lives, and have learned caution and reverence in
deciding upon important points. And there we all sit and listen,
and but few are aware of the fact, and most would think it a
gross exaggeration of terms if one pointed to the immorality of
such a proceeding, if one called it lying and impertinence. Nay,
not in conversation only are these sins committed, but even in
print; and as S uses his impressive personality to give weight
to his unsound information, famous men use their reputation
to commit this sin against the sanctity of truth and honest work.

"How could you, my friend, live with a person whose whole
scale of truthfulness and thought was absolutely different from
yours? There would be no common language between you,
there would really be no common moral basis, as little as there
exists between an Arab chief and a refined English girl. You
know I do not care for Blue-stockings, and that they do not
attract me. But, my dear friend, never marry a fool or a woman
whose intellectual sense of truth is not refined. Not only her
power of reasoning, but her power of sympathy will be un-
developed. She will never be able to ignore her desires when
they are governed by her feeling. There will be no ultimate
judge to appeal to when feeling loses its correct bearings and is
bedimmed or polluted by passion great or small.

"And how can this great virtue be taught, or can it be taught
at all? I believe it can in many ways, but especially in one.
You know how I have always argued and fought against the
current notion that the natural sciences could supplant and
replace the study of the humanities. You know how I have
argued against the predominance of the so-called useful professional studies, and in favour of the studies that aim, above
all, at culture and refinement of taste. I have done this, even

running into the paradoxical. Well, now I wish to extol the natural sciences, and to accentuate their educational value. It is to them chiefly, and to their development and diffusion in modern times, that we owe this refinement of the sense of truth, theoretical and *practical*. I do not mean to attach so much importance to the acquisition of the rudiments of chemistry and physics, to the learning of formulas, to the familiarization of the chief results of natural history, of biology, and zoology. This I consider comparatively unimportant. But I wish all people at some period of their education, to learn and realize how, by what method, after what careful and conscientious process of induction, these general truths are arrived at. They are to read Darwin, that great life-work of a truly modest and charitable man, not so much to know what evolution is, or to speculate on the origin of species, but to learn, by personal, emotional experience, in living through another man's unselfish work, how much careful weighing of numberless instances, and the elimination of the personal selfish desire to see things as one desires to see them, it requires before one is justified in expressing an opinion or even in forming one for one's self. A man or a woman who has realized this fully once in his or her life will be not only wider and of keener perception ever after, but will be morally improved, more just and charitable, more self-forgetful, and more helpful to others—they will be higher social beings.

"*O Sancta Modestia, Filia Veritatis....* You see, I must talk Latin; we have no word to convey the idea of this gracious virtue. The prurient people have robbed the noble word modesty from us, and have restricted, lowered and weakened its meaning."

I have but very inadequately given what my friend said that evening. All his eloquence has been lost in my transcription, and the surroundings, the *milieu* of his panegyric of modesty, I cannot at all render. The quiet of the college court at midnight, the scholastic and still modern sense of seclusion of the college rooms, the friend with face lighted up as by inspiration, his head bent forward as if in eagerness to convey the whole truth, while he paced up and down, occasionally pausing when he felt the truth coming to him—the absence of all this must diminish the impressiveness of my account.

It became quite a turning-point in my own way of looking at things and people. I traced it everywhere, felt the beauty of its presence, and the ugliness and distress where it was not.

No, we have not now one word that conveys this simple virtue fully and adequately. The French have *modestie*, and the Germans have *Bescheidenheit*; but our word *modesty* has lost its original strength; it has been narrowed down and weakened into one special groove of meaning, until it corresponds more to the French word *pudeur*, the German *Schamgefühl* and seems to do duty for the words *chastity* and *purity*, or sense of shame, the meanings of which it is meant to convey in a weakened and more acceptable form.

There seems to be a constant direction of change in the history of words amounting almost to what might be called a law. They seem to lose their strength, and their keen edge of meaning with use. They either become vulgarized, or caricatured, or modified into social levity, and when once they have thus degenerated they lie fallow for a long time, until occasionally, when the commonness of over-use or abuse has died out of memory, they may be revived, as an archaic term by some writer of literary note, and then resume their pristine strength of meaning.

There are many causes for this process of degeneration of words. One very powerful cause is the tendency towards euphemism—towards softening down meanings that may be shocking to tender sensibilities or unpleasant in their associations. Then a word of kindred meaning is taken from another sphere, becomes fixed by use to this indirect meaning, and in its turn loses its early strength of significance. Chastity and purity appeared too strong for ordinary social use, and thus modesty has been more and more employed to convey this narrow or weaker meaning of delicacy of thought and manners. But we want its original strength back to designate the cardinal virtue my friend valued so highly.

The modest man and the modest woman are those who possess the true humility of heart and mind which lies midway between arrogance and aggressive assurance on the one hand and mock-humility and morbid diffidence on the other. The modest man is the one who takes the true and just estimate of himself and of his views and opinions, and lives and speaks up to the standard of this just estimate, neither above nor below it. But the difficult question is that of determining what is this just estimate. Well, it is not to be found in the unsound comparison of one's self with others, but lies in the fullest conception of all the faculties that are imperfect in one's self—in the ideal of one's own best powers. Whoever holds such higher views of a possible self before him will be humble of his own attainments on the one hand, and dignified in the self-dependence which admits of no pharisaical self-gratulation or servile self-obliteration on the other. And so with thoughts and convictions and opinions which will be judged of by the divine ideals of knowledge and of goodness.

But it is still safer to keep these ideals before one's eyes and not to waste one's energies in looking inward too much. Our own importance is never very great, and is most likely to make itself felt in its fullest power the more we merge all the energies its contemplation might consume into the struggle for the attainment of what is highest and best.

What does it all mean, and what have I meant by writing this? I mean to show the importance of intellectual honesty *practised* continuously and constantly, even in the smallest everyday occurrence, until it becomes a necessary habit of mind, a natural instinct, a moving or guiding power to every beat of our heart. It is true "the good heart" is at the bottom of even our most superficial virtue or social grace. But what I wish to accentuate here is the educational importance of this intellectual modesty in forming or maintaining the good heart. The old-fashioned Biblical term, "the bad heart," means pride, and pride is want of true modesty, and modesty we learn when we realize fully how hard it is to grasp truth, and how careful we must be in allowing ourselves to form an opinion.

Reprinted from *The Nineteenth Century and After*, Jan. 1919.

APPENDIX V.

THE KAISER AND "THE WILL TO..."

THE NEED FOR UNIVERSAL RECONSTRUCTION OF MORALS.

I

ONE of the minor manifestations of the prevailing Teutonic spirit which led to this War is to be found in the invention of a comparatively new phrase and its constant use by those who were directly responsible for the War in the period preceding its outbreak and throughout the whole of its duration.

The phrases—"the Will to Deeds" (*der Wille zur Tat*), "the Will to Might," "the Will to Victory," "the Will to Unity," even "the Will to Defeat," or, as ascribed to their enemies, "the Will to Destruction," occurred in nearly every pronouncement or speech made by the Kaiser, his statesmen and generals since 1907 The constant reiteration of such phrases and what they imply, and their continuous repercussion upon the ear of the public, not only of the German people, but of their enemies and of neutrals, have so thoroughly familiarised the world with this unusual and illogical phrase (which, moreover, runs counter to the vernacular character of the German as well as of the English language), that similar phrases have found their way into our own language in these latter days or, at least, into that insidiously dangerous and demoralising sphere of our language, the "Journalese."

A critical investigation of the meaning, origin and import of these phrases will repay some attention; and will not only throw light upon the origin and conduct of this monstrously irrational and immoral War, but also upon the all-important problem of the future reconstruction of civilised society, far beyond the ordinary weight which we might attach to a mere phrase.

That before our days the use of the word "will" in an abstract, almost cosmical, significance, beyond its designation of one of the several faculties of the human mind, is contrary to the significance attached to it in ordinary vernacular, will hardly be disputed. Still less usual, and still more contrary to the spirit of our thought and language, is its use as a substantive, with the preposition "to" immediately governing another substantive, though the substantive may imply some form of activity.

The form in which it has hitherto been used—and rightly used—is to govern some verb expressive of the definite activity arising out of the will or directed by it. We thus have a will to act, to rest, to work, to play, to fight, to give in, etc. It clearly denotes that one of our several faculties is directed towards a definite action; the more definite and individual the action, the more clearly does this human power manifest its nature and strength and the clearer is the meaning conveyed; the vaguer and more confused, general and abstract, the less clear becomes the meaning to be conveyed, until it ends in nonsense. Thus we may have a will to fight, and we generally do fight to win; but we do not add to the clearness of expression by maintaining that we are generally moved by the "will to victory." The phrase may imply a whole world of activities and consequences and of implied meaning, and is either a platitude or a confused mystical suggestion clad in the garb of bombastic rhetoric. Still more is this the case when the German word "will" is not applied to the individual human mind, but to the collective mind of a whole nation. Even then this German phrase does not end there in its comprehensive pretentiousness. It connotes beyond and above the human mind—not the Divine will—but some kind of cosmical force infused into the world of nature and of mankind by human intelligence. It is thus raised to the dignity of a metaphysical principle, however much it may be flattened out and lowered down to the practical use of the market-place, the political stump speaker's platform, the barracks' drillyard and the world's battlefields. As a matter of fact, as we shall see, it thus has its primary, though more remote, origin in the metaphysics of Schopenhauer, the title of which is *Die Welt als Wille und Vorstellung*.

In Schopenhauer's system the word "will" conveys the widely metaphysical meaning corresponding to force, to emotive power in some degree cognate to the ancient Greek Hesiodic conception of Eros or Love (not the later boy—Cupid), the oldest of gods, the force out of which the world grew. Still more remote and more vaguely influential was the Hegelian conception of the State as a fixed and final entity in the life of humanity, above reason and morality, which has to some degree led to the establishment by German publicists of their conception of the State and to the rule of German *Politismus* by publicists and political writers. At all events, whether vaguely suggested or clearly apprehended by those who have used this modern phrase, the suggestion of such an extra-human or cosmical conception is conveyed in their use of the term "will."

Now we have always been aware of the importance of will and will-power, not only in the formation of perfect human character, but also in its effect upon achieving human design and purpose in the usual world of events and things about us. Will-power has always been and will ever remain one of the chief factors in human life. With some poetic license and in the form of epigrammatic exaggeration in order to impress our meaning, we have always insisted upon the power of the will to achieve whatever purpose it sets itself: "Where there's a will there's a way" is one of the oldest commonplaces in our language. The supreme importance of concentration of thought and action, of rapid resolution or continuous perseverance, of energy, and of conviction which underlies the concentrated energy to act—all these conceptions have been admitted and emphasised as principles guiding our life and as injunctions in the preparation for life in our education. Wordsworth praises

> The reason firm, the temperate will,
> Endurance, foresight, strength, and skill.

In our conception of will the human faculty is always co-ordinated with the other factors of human intellect and character. Above all, it is subordinated to the wider ethical and social elements of reason and morality. Will divorced from these is either mere animal instinct or passion. In civilised society we soon learn to respect the will of others while asserting our own independence, and both wills are subject to justice and truth.

However much we may respond to the will of others, this spirit of freedom and justice in us will never subject itself to arbitrariness or license on the part of others. In the words of Sir Henry Wotton:

> How happy is he born and taught
> That serveth not another's will,
> Whose armour is his honest thought
> And simple truth his utmost skill.

In our civilised life the universally accepted principles of social morality, which underlie the individual will and the collective will of nations and of mankind, are based, not only upon reason and justice, but upon love or charity as well. The motive force in man, whether instinct or passion, energy or self-realisation, is inseparably interwoven with these principles, which act as the directing power to such vital energy. In the imaginary world we can only conceive of one sphere where reason and justice leave the will uncontrolled, and where love is replaced by hate, namely —in Hell. It is Lucifer who gives supremely beautiful expression to the principles ruling his domain:

> What though the field be lost?
> All is not lost; the unconquerable Will,
> And study of revenge, immortal hate,
> And courage never to submit or yield[1].

What governs the individual will also applies to the collective will of the State or Sovereign. In the States composed of freemen, Democracy, in the conception of the ancient Greeks and of the free people of our own times,

> Men their duties know,
> But know their rights, and knowing dare maintain.
>
> .   .   .   .   .   .
>
> And sovereign law, that State's collected will,
> O'er thrones and globes elate,
> Sits empress, crowning good, repressing ill.
>
> (Sir William Jones.)

But, in the sham-cosmical conception of will in the phrases as used by the Kaiser and his learned or unlearned henchmen, his own will or the will of the State and the German nation is

---

[1] *Paradise Lost*, i. 105.

divorced from reason, justice and charity, as the State and the sovereign are supreme and are raised above morality. Might becomes right, and the "will to might" is the dominating principle of State action and of the citizens composing the State. These principles embody the latter-day system of morality dominating the political and social life of the German people, which led to this War and which established the barbarous methods by which it was carried on. They differ as much from the principles regulating the life of the older Germany as the ethics of Kant differ from those of Nietzsche. It required nearly fifty years for the Nietzschean ethics to percolate to such a degree through the moral consciousness of the German people, and for the German publicists, writers and teachers to pave the way for the Kaiser with his bureaucrats and militarists to advance to those heights of popular influence from which he could make the most definite practical application of these principles in order to lead Germany to world-dominion.

In tracing the widespread introduction of these definite phrases, we are able to fix the exact date when, by supreme sanction of the Over-Lord, they are used as a watchword for the political regeneration of his people and for the establishment of Pan-Germanism throughout the world. The first time the Kaiser used such a phrase was in his Speech from the Throne at the opening of the Reichstag in February of 1907. His peroration ran thus:

And now, gentlemen, may our national sentiment and our Will to Deeds (*Wille zur Tat*), out of which this Reichstag has sprung, also dominate its work—for the salvation of Germany.

When we recall the Willy-Nicky telegrams of 1904–5, the phrase might have run "Der Wille zum Tag"!

This is, as far as I can ascertain, the first time that the phrase was used in a public pronouncement. The Kaiser's use of the phrase is thus the first application of this more or less philosophical term for definite practical purposes in the political life of the German nation. The date 1907, when taken in connexion with the general trend of international politics of those days, is most significant. "The Day" (*der Tag*) was already a watchword in the Army and Navy. From that time onwards it recurs

again and again in German political speeches, especially in
reference to the foreign policy of the German nation and its
need for expansion; until, during the period immediately preceding the War, and also during the War, hardly any speech
has been made by the civil and military authorities without the
obtrusion of some reference to the "Will to war," "to victory,"
"to power," etc.

We have already indicated by anticipation the source whence
this form of expression, and the idea it conveys, are derived.
Ultimately, it originates in the philosophical writings of
Schopenhauer, combined with the theories of Hegel concerning
the State, its nature, and its powers—especially in Schopenhauer. But directly it owes its origin to Nietzsche, whose
brilliant literary expositions as, perhaps, the greatest of German
writers of passionate prose, effectually familiarised the wider
public with the phrase and the ideas it conveys in every class
of German society.

The truth of this statement will be admitted by the German
authorities themselves. Georg Büchmann, in his popular book
Geflügelte Worte (edition of 1912), in dealing with the phrase
"*der Wille zur Tat*" (the Will to Deeds or to Action), says:
"The forging of this term, first used in Nietzsche's *Richard
Wagner in Bayreuth* (1876), was beyond all question influenced
by Schopenhauer's *Die Welt als Wille und Vorstellung*." As we
maintained above, Schopenhauer's use of the term "will" and,
even in its application to human life, the phrase "the Will to
Life" (*der Wille zum Leben*), partake more of an abstract and
metaphysical significance.

In Nietzsche, however, it is directly concerned with man's
social and moral attitude towards his fellow-men, and aims at
becoming a direct and fundamental guide to moral (or, rather,
unmoral) human existence. With him the phrase is essentially
connected with his theory of the Superman. This term, so much
used of late years in every part of the world, did not originate
with Nietzsche. In fact it goes back to the ancient Greek poets,
to Homer and Hesiod and to Lucian, in whom the terms
ὑπερηνορέων, ὑπερήνωρ and ὑπεράνθρωπος occur. In Seneca we
have the phrase "*supra hominem est.*" In German the term

"*Uebermensch*," besides occurring in the writings of Hippel, Jean Paul, Grabbe, and others, is found in two famous passages in Goethe's *Faust*. Goethe probably derived his use of the term from Herder, who again borrowed it from the numerous theological writers of the seventeenth, eighteenth and nineteenth centuries. These theological writers used the term in a very different—in fact, in an opposite, significance to that attached to it by Nietzsche. Thus in a Book of Devotions of the seventeenth century by Heinrich Müller we read that "in the new man thou art a true man, a superman, a man of God, and a Christian man" (*Im neuen Menschen bist Du ein wahrer Mensch, ein Ober-Mensch, ein Gottes- und Christen-Mensch*). The term is used in various forms with the same significance in other devotional literature, once even as early as in a letter by the Saxon Dominican Hermann Rab, dated 1527, down to the nineteenth century. In this last instance it is even applied to the Saviour Himself in a book published anonymously in Berlin in 1807, "The Life of the Superman Jesus, the Christ, the Great Man from Palestine" (*Lebenslauf des Ober-menschen Jesus des Christus des Grossen Mannes aus Palästina*).

Now, Nietzsche's conception of the Superman is vastly different from that of these theological writers. To quote Büchmann's admirable summary[1]:

The term Superman has only become a commonplace in the modern sense through Nietzsche, who sees in him a forceful being to whom nothing is good but what he wills and who overthrows ruthlessly whatsoever opposes him. No doubt the conception of "Rulers-morality" and of the "Blond Beast" was introduced by others. Nietzsche himself saw in the Superman only a higher ideal step made by humanity, which was thus to develop in the same degree as is found in the step from animal to man. In his most popular book, *Also sprach Zarathustra* (1883), he says: "I teach to you the Superman. Man is something that must be overcome. All beings have hitherto created something above themselves; and you wish to remain the ebb of this great flood-tide, and rather to return to the animal than to overcome man? What is the ape to man? Laughter and painful shame; and just so man is to be to the Superman—'laughter and painful shame.'"

[1] *Geflügelte Worte*, p. 262.

In spite of Büchmann's attempt to attribute to others the conception of "Rulers-morality" and of the "Blond Beast," he himself refers to the undoubted introduction of these terms by Nietzsche in his Essay *Beyond Good and Evil* (1886), where he asserts that there exists "a morality for Rulers, and a Morality for Slaves" (*Es gibt Herren-moral und Sklaven-moral*); and further maintains that "morality in Europe is to-day the morality of herded animals" (*Moral ist heute Herdentier-moral*). Furthermore, in his Essay on the *Genealogy of Morals* (1887) (probably influenced by de Gobineau), he refers to the "need of all aristocratic races" to compensate themselves for the social constraint, which in times of Peace they must impose upon themselves, by means of cruelty to other races; and thus, as exulting monsters, to return to the innocence of the predatory animals (*Raubtier Gewissen*), as the glorious "Blond Beast," lustfully roaming about in search of prey and victory; and this term of the Blond Beast especially refers to the German nation as that of the Blond Germanic Beast (*Blonde Germanische Bestie*). Nietzsche's last literary effort, begun in 1886, and left unfinished, was posthumously published in 1895. It bears the significant title "The Will to Power" (*Der Wille zur Macht. Versuch einer Umwertung aller Werte*)[1].

[1] No doubt one of the most influential factors in familiarising the German people with the philosophy of Schopenhauer was the widespread popularity of Wagner's Music-dramas, especially *The Ring of the Nibelungen*. Wagner was, during the greater part of his life, a direct and convinced disciple of Schopenhauer, and consciously embodied the leading principles of his philosophy in his own artistic creations. The central figure of Siegfried ("who knew not what fear meant") as a personification of will-power, the only force which rules life, represents his conception of Schopenhauer's Will. How popularly-effective this artistic teaching has been is illustrated by the simple fact, that, after the Hindenburg-line, the chief remaining trench-lines of German defences were all named after these heroes of the "Blond Beast" as embodied in the Wagnerian rendering of Nordic mythology. In addition to the Siegfried-line were the Brünhilde-line, the Hunding-line, the Wotan-line, etc. It is true that in his later life the claims of Christian charity and humility were admitted by Wagner in the creation of the inartistic, undramatic and un-heroic figure of Parsifal. For the *Reine Thor* (the pure dolt, who

Now the influence of such doctrines upon the mentality of the German people, who deliberately began this world-war, and have carried it on with the ruthless bestiality and deceit—not of super-men, but of savage beasts—is so manifest that it requires no further exposition. It must, however, be admitted that, though Nietzsche's ethical philosophy fails chiefly through a complete misunderstanding and misapplication of the Darwinian principle of evolution, there are aspects of it which distinctly make for an advance of the human species. I even venture to believe that he would have been the first to repudiate the policy, and the methods of realising it, adopted by Germany in these latter years, as he would have been horrified by the ruthlessness and treachery which have been displayed. His own estimate of the specific character of German mentality and of German politics was a very low one. I also believe that his own personality, in so far as it was not warped and distorted by his pathological condition ending in insanity, with premonitory symptoms throughout the whole of his life, was refined and noble, actuated throughout by higher beneficent ideals. His works abound in deep and brilliant thoughts, sometimes clearly expressed, but often bedimmed and confused by emotions and pathological impulses over which he had no control, and frequently, if not generally, placed in a setting of irrational and exaggerated diction and reasoning which robbed them of truth and effectiveness. The value of his works, however, rests chiefly upon their literary and artistic qualities, which have ensured the wide popularity which they enjoy. *Zarathustra* will ever remain a masterpiece of German prose; though it contains much crude and nebulous thought—at times even insane nonsense— all the more deleterious to the mind of the reader because of the artistic beauty and force of its diction.

ineptly answers "I do not know") can never impress an audience with his heroic character, any more than sacrifice and humility can be artistically conveyed by mere iteration of their virtues. The great critic Lessing, in the eighteenth century, had already shown that, while the figures of the Old Testament were as dramatic as those of ancient Greek mythology, those of Christian martyrology were essentially undramatic.

Now, it must be admitted to be incontrovertible that the philosophical and ethical writings of Nietzsche have directly produced the phrases indicated in the title of this article and what these phrases imply in regard to the mentality of the German nation. Since the War began, however, frequent attempts have been made in Germany, with a definite political purpose, to deny the great influence which Nietzsche has had upon the mentality of the present generation. We can understand the reasons for such an attempt, but we do not admit its truth. It would be difficult to find any book which has enjoyed such enormous popularity in Germany as *Zarathustra*. I can only record my own personal experiences during the occasional visits I paid to Germany in the 'nineties of the last century. I then found that among many of the young men, and even the young women, whom I met, Nietzschean ideas of morality were widely prevalent and were actually adopted as guides to conduct. The same attempt has frequently been made to deny the influence of the writings of Bernhardi, as well as the writings and teachings of Treitschke, whose responsibility in fashioning the mentality of the German nation for this world-war, with its methods of deliberate ruthlessness, has been amply demonstrated by numerous competent writers. Not only in Germany have such attempts been made to minimise their influence, but in neutral countries as well. So, for instance, the reviewer of my book *Aristodemocracy*, etc., in the *New Republic* of New York attempted to refute my own affirmation of the great influence of Treitschke's teaching, and maintained that his *Politik* (I am not aware that he ever published such a book, though his popular lectures on that subject for many years drew large audiences) did not enjoy a wide circulation. My reply to such an assertion was, and is, that all the historical and political writings of Treitschke did have a comparatively wide circulation in Germany, and that, as editor of the *Preussische Jahrbücher*, he had greater facilities for reaching a wider circle of German readers than any other publicist or historian in that country. But it must never be forgotten that a Professor in one of the great German Universities has more direct means of transmitting his opinions throughout the whole nation than in any other country. In the first place, all schoolmasters are obliged to pass a "State examination" in order to follow their profession, and must have attended courses of lectures in the Universities. For at least forty years, thousands of these students attended Treitschke's lectures, thereafter transmitting his opinions and principles among their own pupils of every class and in every part of Germany. But, not only these schoolmasters, jurists, politicians, and bureaucrats, but university students of *every* branch of study were eager listeners of his forceful and eloquent lectures. During the three and a half years (from 1873 to 1876) when I was a student at German universities, I remember how, at Heidelberg, his more popular lectures on *Politik* were attended on an average by about five hundred students from every Faculty, out of a total number of less than a thousand students then attending that University. These numbers were greatly increased after he became a professor at Berlin in 1874 and was made a member of the Reichstag.

It need not be insisted upon how effective such a personal agency for the transmission of opinion and doctrine is in a country with such an effective educational system, in which, moreover, the willing receptivity for intellectual teaching among the whole population is a leading characteristic of decided national advantage. What thus applies to the teachings of Treitschke also applies to the more abstract speculative teaching of pure philosophy, such as that of Hegel, which filters through the mentality of students who become officials or professional men or educated men of affairs, and through them even into the minds of the illiterate persons with whom they come in contact and over whom they have some influence. Moreover, it was especially the class to which the average schoolmaster belonged which consisted of the most faithful readers of Nietzsche and became his most ardent disciples.

II

The foregoing remarks on the philosophic and ethical systems prevailing in Germany before the War were not made for the purpose of summarising their distinctive characteristics, nor even of proving that they had a considerable influence in producing this war. Similar attempts have already been made by several competent writers.

My chief central aim in this article has been to illustrate with emphasis, by means, in the first instance, of the origin and frequent application of that unusual and popular phrase "The Will to...," the direct and most effective influence of the highest abstract theory and philosophy upon the mentality and the actual life of a whole nation. That the German people is thus peculiarly receptive to such an intellectual and moral process, is probably true; and, whatever their most reprehensible weaknesses and vices may be, this remains one of their chief qualities and virtues as a nation. But it would be the greatest and most vital error to believe that they represent a unique instance of this national characteristic among the nations of our day, or of any other period in history. Every nation is thus influenced by the supreme expression of philosophic and religious thought in the generation preceding it, and in its contemporary life. Philosophy holds the mirror of intellectuality, of thought, of principles and motives before the eyes of the peoples of each age. Its immediate function is—to use the language of our enemies—to bring their *Zeitgeist*, their Time-Spirit, to the consciousness of the people. It is more than a platitude to maintain that "to know thyself" is the first step towards rational and beneficent action and progress. The higher the civilisation and the more real the true democracy, the greater is the effectiveness and power of such a *Zeitgeist*, as well as the need for its correct formulation, and the more direct becomes its action. With the growing diffusion of knowledge, since the invention of the printing press and other inventions which have facilitated rapid transportation and inter-communication, the gap between the formulation of truth and higher ideas and ideals, on the one hand, and their realisation in the life of a whole nation, on the other, becomes shortened and effectually bridged over. This has been the case in the past, and will be still more so in the future. In mediaeval society the Church was mainly effective in performing this supreme purpose of national education. The doctrines and dogmas of the Church, as well as its ethical teaching, were transmitted, not only through the ordained and authoritative priests, but through that wide and influential class called "clerks," i.e. those possessed of letters and learning among the mass of the illiterates. Throughout the whole world there was a vast fraternity of the learned linked together into effective unity by one universal language, Latin. In the whole history of civilisation, no three men more fully understood and appreciated the value of true philosophy, morality and religion, and especially the direct and supreme force of education, than did Erasmus, Sir Thomas More, and Colet. Their conception of a true reformation was entirely based upon Humanism, beginning with the clerks, and, through them, of all the peoples of Christendom. If this were true in the age of the Reformation, it is true to a still greater and more intense degree in our own immediate age, the Great Age of Reformation for the future.

But if we are right in ascribing such direct power to what, in one word, we must call Philosophy, it becomes still more urgently true that the highest exposition of our "Time-Spirit" should be the right one, the true philosophy, the true morality. For it was the false philosophy (or at least the distorted understanding and application of the true philosophy) which has brought ruin to Germany and unspeakable disaster to the world. Above all, our system of morals must not lag behind the consciousness and the needs of our age; but must, on the contrary, summarise what is best in the conception of our higher ideals, and prepare for, facilitate and accelerate progress in the direction of these ideals. This is the primary and essential requisite for a Moral Reconstruction of our age, and for the preparation of a glorious new age for posterity.

In spite of the many national virtues of which the British people, with all due modesty, may be justly proud, it is in this sphere of public life and of national education that we are singularly at fault. Our national spirit of conservatism, coupled with our keen appreciation of the actualities of life, of experience, of the unbiassed use of common-sense in dealing with the facts and problems before us, our straightforward energy, courage and perseverance in facing the difficulties to be overcome, as we faced our enemies in fight, our consequent hatred of sham and of cant (whether patently manifest or hidden in the garb of rhetoric or deep philosophy)—all these, and much more, have made us suspicious of abstractions, of higher thought, theory and philosophy, until at times we even hate or despise them. These are the facts which led Meredith to summarise this national idiosyncrasy in the phrase "England's Hatred of Thought." This is true in spite of our having actually produced, perhaps, the greatest individual thinkers of the world. Not so the French with their courageous, nay, passionate, almost artistic, love of ideas, of new ideas, and their child-like exuberance and boldness in at once daring to carry them into realisation with heedless and fearless disregard of the existing order of things. Not so the Germans with their love of systematic thought, their almost mystic and romantic attachment to deductive generalisation, and their patient docility in penetrating and marshalling the world of facts in their true order under the supremacy of a regulating and dominating idea. The idea and the system become great realities to them, and they exact submission to their autocratic sway, as for many generations they have been trained to obedience to their master and their over-lords in their political and social life. Civil obedience and military discipline may bear supremely good fruit when in peace we have the perfect benevolent and sane autocrat, and in war the courageously wise and wisely energetic general. In the spiritual world of the mind and character the persuasive rule of true philosophy also becomes a wholly beneficent autocrat.

If Germany has suffered, and still suffers, from the tyranny of its false philosophy, we suffer, and will suffer, from the absence of any philosophy.

I cannot refrain from recording my own personal impressions of the national characteristics with which we are dealing. When, more than forty-two years ago, I settled in this country, having been born and bred in America, and having studied for over three years at German Universities, what struck me most as the leading and national characteristic of this country and its people, in contradistinction to that of the German people among whom I had been living—to summarise it in one phrase—was "The Force of Tradition." Tradition was all-powerful, and could only be modified by a process of organic evolution, in no way manifestly subject to even those leading thinkers and workers who might directly or indirectly have effected the evolutionary change or given it direction. In Germany and also in France, and even in the United States in certain departments, the process of change and innovation was directly identified with some leading personality and his work. But in Germany it was the philosopher and professor; in France the political writer and orator, as well as the poet, the man of letters; and in the United States, it was chiefly the business-man. In England the great formative causes appear to me to be the political traditions, more or less adequately represented by parliamentary parties, and the national institutions and customs arising out of the continuous life of the people and re-acting upon it. By a natural process, if not a "Social Law," the occupations which conferred the greatest social distinction and prestige attracted to themselves eventually, both in quality and in quantity, the talent of a nation or of a community: so, at least in those golden days of the immediate past, politics seemed to attract the talent and genius of England, as it also conveyed the greatest influence and prestige. In the Germany of those days the universities and the army conferred the same prestige. As years went by, the army encroached upon the universities with the Bureaucracy holding a good second between them. But in England I was chiefly struck with this directly effective "force of tradition" in the customs emanating from, or grouping round, the different communal and social organisa-tions and their manifest corporate bodies; and this was so in both serious work and lighter play. As regards the latter, the whole world of sport, with its varied manifestations in all forms of physical enjoyment and its corporate organisation, appeared to be, and appears so still, one of the most potent formative elements in giving direction to the social life of the entire com-munity, as well as to the character of public morals. I have more than once in the past (a year and a half ago in the pages of this Review)[1] insisted on the supreme influence of athletics, the sports and pastimes of England, upon the character of the British people. May the good that is in them always survive and be retained for the welfare of the English nation and of the British Empire!

In all these organisations the immediate force of tradition is supreme and manifest. It applies, not only to the various County teams and Clubs, which are good or bad as their corporate character and atmosphere are confirmed or maintained or changed by gradual and imperceptible evolution; but in every other corporate body. Schools and universities with their houses and colleges, ships and regiments, and even their companies, boroughs and counties with their several organisations for work and play, societies and clubs, even factories and the business firms, are all ruled by certain traditions, firmly established and directly effective, advancing or degenerating by a gradual process, the immediate personal origin of which may not always be distinguishable,—but all of them subject to the Force of Tradition. Now this is a great force and a great asset to a nation, if its effectiveness tends to the good; but it may become a weakness, a stumbling-block to improvement and progress, a negation even of the original purpose for which the corporate body was called into existence. If it tends to the bad, still more so if the tendency is clearly evil, even if the activity and the tradition by which it is dominated and directed no longer conform to the actual need of the social life in which the corporate body acts, the slow and organic process of change has its undoubted advantages. But in this long and halting period of adaptation intervening between a crying need and its realisation or amendment, much irreparable harm may be done and suffering undergone. "*On a toujours les défauts de ses qualités*" is undoubtedly true. 'But in spite of the *qualities*, the *faults* remain faults, and may be most maleficent. We must see to it that the forces which fashion our national life, whether by tradition or by conscious design, theory, and law, harmonise

[1] See the *Nineteenth Century and After* for December, 1916, "The Social Gulf between England and Germany," and April, 1917, "Morality and German War Aims."

with the consciousness of the age in which we live, respond to the needs of the actual times, and, above all, prepare the way for a better future.

Now, if I have succeeded in showing how direct is the influence which German philosophical theories of ethics had in the making of Germany, and in producing this world-war and its methods of warfare, we can realise how, even among other nations, including ourselves, the theoretical foundations of national consciousness and morals are of supreme importance and effectiveness. Above all must we realise how supremely important it is that our ethical philosophy should be the right one. It is because of this that "Moral Reconstruction" constitutes the most crying need of our age, not only for Germany, but throughout the world, and especially so in this country[1].

I wish at once to make it quite clear that, though I hold (and have endeavoured in *Aristodemocracy* to prove it) that ethics and religion, never divorced, can never replace each other, I am equally convinced that religion, which is concerned with man's communion with his ultimate ideals, forms the foundation of moral and intellectual activities and strivings in the whole spiritual life of man. But religion does not then mean merely its doctrinal, sectarian or ritual (in the widest acceptation of the term) manifestations. All philosophy and all science lead up to, and are ultimately based upon, man's religion. But philosophy and science, in their specific development and their application to mental and material life, must be elaborated and advanced independently and with conscientious thoroughness in every age. The same claim must be made with regard to our system of morals.

Now, what may be called the "system of catechismal ethics" is no longer adequate or effectual, first, because the catechism is

---

[1] I have developed my views on this subject in my book *Aristodemocracy from the Great War back to Moses, Christ and Plato* (1916); in *Patriotism, National and International* (1917); *What Germany is Fighting For* (1917); and in the present book of which this article forms an Appendix. Such books as Mr A. Clutton Brock's *The Ultimate Belief*, with its simple and yet exalted style and tone, serve as very useful moral and intellectual stimulants.

overshadowed by doctrinal teaching; and, while therefore confusing the youthful mind in the grasping of the elements of practical ethics of even the believers in the respective sectarian religions, it can in no way become a guide to the non-believers. These latter will therefore often enter life without any ethical instruction whatever. But, in the second place, it is no longer adequate, because each age develops a new form of ethics corresponding to, and completely harmonising with, the phase of social evolution attained, the needs which the actual times produce, and the adaptation to the new conditions of progressive activity in preparing for a future age. It hardly requires lengthy and insistent demonstration to prove to every thoughtful person that the conceptions of truthfulness, honesty and honour, participation in public and political work, etc., etc., differ and advance or decline during the several ages of history, and even within a few generations. Theory and education must therefore keep pace with these historical changes; and it is all-important for national sanity, truthfulness and progress that this should be so.

As regards reconstruction in ethical theory—in spite of the establishment and advance in our times of the study called Sociology—it still remains an urgent necessity that the purely philosophical study of Ethics, pervaded by the highest philosophical spirit and method, should be essentially modified. This modification must take place in one definite direction. Hitherto, the philosophical study of Ethics has been almost exclusively concerned with the fundamental principles on which all Ethics rest, and, if not purely deductive or introspective, metaphysical and psychological, it has not been essentially inductive, observational and experimental—in spite of the fact that Kant distinguished the ethical department from all others in philosophy by assigning to his work on that subject the title *Critique of Practical Reason* in contradistinction to the *Critique of Pure Reason*. The main task for the ethical student of the future will be to discover, establish and formulate, in the purest spirit of philosophy, the actual moral consciousness of the age in which he is living and, on the ground of inductive and thorough observation, and even experiment, to base his ethical generalisation on these. Having performed this primarily necessary task, he can turn back to more complete co-ordination with psychological and metaphysical principles, and push forward to their application in order to produce a more perfect life.

A whole field of vital and interesting study and discussion is opened out to the philosopher—the field of definite inquiry into life, private and public. Hitherto this domain of inquiry has been left to the casual attention of the literary essayist, and even of the poet and novelist, or to the philanthropist and social reformer. The work of the modern novelist, beginning with Dickens, Zola and the American writer, Norris, has often been inspired by the aim to expose great social evils and needs, and to advocate their reform. What is required from the philosophical moralist is, that he should, with all the highly accurate apparatus of his methods, apply himself to the establishment of the dominating and valid ethical principles in the life of his age. Truthfulness, Honour, Honesty (including commercial and political honesty), Cleanliness, Charity—in short the principles guiding human action in every department of modern life—should be established in their adequate modern form by unbiassed and searching observation and inquiry and co-ordinated with the whole ethical system of our days. The controversies turning round the fundamental bases of morality, in the metaphysical or psychological spirit, whether it be idealism, realism, egoism or altruism, are not to absorb the whole or the greater part of his study and work; but the actual establishment, for instance, of commercial and industrial morality, in the practices of finance and the Stock Exchange, the promoting and the working of great Stock Companies and syndicates, the differences between investment and speculation on margin, etc., etc., these and similar problems should be subjected to the most thorough and unbiassed ethical investigation by men best fitted for such work by natural ability and thorough training. So, too, the duties of the citizen (which I am pleased to record have already received considerable attention from competent thinkers and writers) are to be impressed upon the people in all phases of public education. These and innumerable other instances are those which truly concern us in our times; and in a simple and intelligible form are to be summarised so that they can be brought home to the average understanding and can be effectually incorporated in our educational system. Catechismal ethics leave us entirely in the dark on these important issues in modern life. The moral consciousness of the public must be brought up to date.

Now, leaving the theoretical side, we finally come to the practical department of education. It would be unfair and disingenuous were I, from the outset, to be met by the commonplace and superficial objection: that knowledge of ethical terms or of ethical practical principles conveyed in text-books, cannot of themselves make a man good; as mere learning cannot make a man wise. But even Nature's wise man is not turned into a fool by being made acquainted, in his early or later education, with the rudiments of learning and science, which affect the whole of our civilisation. Reading and writing, grammar and arithmetic, history and geography, will not destroy the intellect and its efficiency of even a man born with mother-wit and brain-power and possessed of ordinary common-sense. The child favoured at birth with a nature tending towards virtue, kindliness and strength of character ought to be instructed in what the society about him considers right and wrong, and ought not to be left to his instincts and passions. More than this, he must be made acquainted with the highest prevailing moral tenets of his own age. This the catechisms of the present day as published by every one of the religious sects cannot do adequately. Above all, it is necessary to remember that a large proportion of children in our large towns and country villages do not attend Sunday school, and are not even instructed in existing catechisms. Nor have they homes in which, by definite instruction or by commendable example, their morals are instilled and improved. To suggest but one instance, the supreme duty to be truthful. In millions of cases this fundamental injunction has never been adequately and convincingly impressed upon the child, either in town or country. It remains one of the most crying needs that modern and thoroughly adequate and efficient Ethics and Civics be taught, and that every citizen be, at some period of education, instructed in the morals of his own age. It goes without saying that such instruction should not be philosophical or theoretical, but eminently simple and practical, that abstractions and generalisations be avoided, and that every injunction be brought home by telling instances and illustrations appealing to the personalities of the pupils. Honour and Truthfulness, Manliness and Courage, Cleanliness of body and of mind, Industry and Self-control, Generosity and Thrift, Public Duty and Public Spirit, can and must thus be inculcated in the young and developed in the adult population. Every teacher of average intelligence will be competent to do this, as well as every clergyman or minister. All sects are surely agreed with regard to such moral injunctions; but the clergyman or minister must appear in the school as the teacher of the Ethics which are universally admitted, and not as the upholder of a definite set of religious doctrines, which might antagonise, or exclude from his teaching, the pupils who are to be instructed in the Civics and Ethics of a civilised community. "By their fruits shall ye know them"; and such fruits will come abundantly to the nation which cultivates both fruit and flower in its national life.

This is one of the most vital needs of National Reconstruction, and, if not more pressing than our economic reconstruction, is at least of equal importance with it for the future health, peace and progress of the Empire.

THE END

For EU product safety concerns, contact us at Calle de José Abascal, 56–1°,
28003 Madrid, Spain or eugpsr@cambridge.org.

www.ingramcontent.com/pod-product-compliance
Ingram Content Group UK Ltd.
Pitfield, Milton Keynes, MK11 3LW, UK
UKHW020318140625
459647UK00018B/1927